Advocacy
Second Edition

Advocacy Second Edition explains how to win cases in court. David Ross QC shows how the most successful advocates do it. This edition examines in great detail the art and techniques of the best of them.

Writing in simple, clear language he gives the benefit of his many years of local and international experience. He describes:

- how to hold a court's attention
- how to start and stop a witness

- how to cross-examine all types of people, from liars to experts
- how to take objections
- how to address a jury
- how to follow etiquette and behave ethically
- how to win impossible cases.

All the principles and tactics are explained, from the striking start to knowledge of the law. All are illustrated by examples taken from real cases.

The second edition of *Advocacy* updates the law. In his easy style, David Ross QC introduces new advice about:

- how to prepare for, and run, an appeal
- how to write effective submissions to a court.

Advocacy Second Edition is essential for both beginning and experienced advocates. It will fascinate anyone who wants to know how the best lawyers operate and how they win their cases.

David Ross QC is an eminent advocate with extensive experience in trials and appeals. He has taught advocacy in many countries.

Praise for the first edition:

"There is no superfluous material, expression is always both economic and precise, and the results are always instructive. The style of the book manifests the qualities of the advocacy it teaches." David J. A. Cairns, Cambridge Law Journal

"This book represents the latest and most extensive work in advocacy teaching. It is essential reading for advocates of all levels of experience." Greg Laughton SC

"There is something here for every practising advocate (and some pleasure for those of us nearing the end). . . . I wish I had written this book." Rex Wild QC

Advocacy
Second Edition

DAVID ROSS QC

CAMBRIDGE
UNIVERSITY PRESS

CAMBRIDGE UNIVERSITY PRESS
Cambridge, New York, Melbourne, Madrid, Cape Town, Singapore, São Paulo

Cambridge University Press
477 Williamstown Road, Port Melbourne, VIC 3207, Australia

Published in the United States of America by Cambridge University Press, New York

www.cambridge.org
Information on this title: www.cambridge.org/9780521884761

First published 2005
Reprinted 2005
Second edition published 2007

Printed in Australia by Ligare

A catalogue record for this publication is available from the British Library

National Library of Australia Cataloguing in Publication data
    Ross, David, QC.
    Advocacy
    2nd ed.
    Includes index.
    ISBN 978-0-521-88476-1 (pbk.)
    1. Trial practice – Australia.   2. Examination of witnesses – Australia.
    3. Legal etiquette – Australia.   I Title.
347.94052

ISBN 978-0-521-88476-1 paperback

Contents

Foreword   *page* xi

1   The nature of advocacy   1
    The essence of advocacy   1
    The qualities of advocacy   1
    The qualities of an advocate   2
    Cases won on admissible evidence   4
    How and what to learn   5
    Good habits   7
    Duties of the advocate   9
    Perfection is not possible   10

2   Preparation   11
    General   11
    The court   11
    Case concept   12
    Never mark a document   13
    Document assembly   13
    Indexing the case   13
    Charts, diagrams and drawings   15
    Photo albums   15
    Additional materials   16
    Three examples   17
    Requirements for litigation   18
    Elements and evidence   18
    Preparing cross-examination   20
    Child witnesses   20
    Admissions   21
    During the trial   22
    Luck   22

3   Witnesses and questions   23
    Witnesses   23
    Witness statements   23
    Choosing which witnesses to call   23
    Civilian witnesses   24
    Practised witnesses   25

Witnesses who make a mistake 26
Witnesses who lie 26
Hostile witnesses 27
Questions 27
Use simple English 27
Never "the accused" 28
One issue to each question 29
Avoid negative questions 29
No padding 30
Never argue with a witness 30
Timing 31
Leading questions 31
Leading questions to avoid 32
Do not comment on an answer 33
When a witness needs an interpreter 34
Watching the witness and listening 34
Demeanour: even temper and politeness 35

4 Examination-in-chief 36
Proof of the case 36
Defence witnesses 36
Level of detail 37
No leading questions 37
The Bolster rule 38
Watching the witness and listening 38
Setting the witness at ease 39
Forms of questions 40
Stopping and starting a witness 41
The right order 42
Refreshing memory 43
Toning down weak points 45
Good character 46
Summary 46

5 Cross-examination: its qualities 48
The nature of cross-examination 48
Is it necessary? 48
Main aims 49
Relevance 50
The rule in *Browne v Dunn* 51
Watch the witness 52
Leading questions 53
Forms of question 55
"Closing the gates" and "tightening the net" 58
Knowing when to stop and how 59
One question too many 59

6 Cross-examination: method and style 60
No one correct technique 60
Confrontation 60
Drawing out every damaging detail 62

Undermining a witness   63
Undermining one witness through another   65
Earlier failure to identify   68
Circumstantial evidence   68
Previous convictions   70
Bad reputation   72
Child witnesses   73
The witness who always agrees   73
Invention and recent invention   73
Summary   74

7   Cross-examination of experts   76
Opinion evidence   76
Is the witness an expert?   77
Cross-examining   78
Proving mistakes   79
Using the simple example   80
Asking one expert about the opinion of another   80
Turning the witness your way   82
Not testing important items   83
Not looking at contemporary notes   85
The expert with bias   85

8   Cross-examination on documents   87
Best and worst aspects   87
Some rules   88
Calling for a document   89
Cross-examining on inadmissible documents   90
Using a document to discredit a witness   91
Prior inconsistent statement   92
Prior inconsistent statement turned to prior consistent
statement   93
Cutting off any escape   94
Summary   97

9   Re-examination   100
The nature of re-examination   100
Is it necessary?   100
Arising from cross-examination   102
No leading questions   103
Explaining the reason   104
Rebutting recent invention   105
Reviving credit   106
Re-examining on documents   106
Summary   106

10 Admissibility, objections and submissions   108
Admissibility   108
Facts in issue   109
Proof   110
Circumstantial cases   112

Objections 113
 Objections to evidence 113
 Objections to forms of questions 115
Submissions 116
 Unfair hearing or abuse of process 116
 No case to answer 116
 Submissions at the end of the case 117
 Legal submissions generally 117
 Recommendations on a no case submission 118

11 The addresses 119
 Addresses generally 119
 Opening address 120
  Civil cases 120
  Criminal cases 120
 Closing address 122
  The essence of advocacy 122
 Prosection closing 123
  The striking start 123
  Disparaging the defence case 124
 Defence closing 124
  Planning 124
  Knowledge of human affairs 124
  Expert evidence 125
  The homely example 126
  Summary 127

12 Plea in mitigation 129
 Introduction 129
 Preparation 130
 The decision on how to plead 131
 Negotiating the lowest charge 131
 Settling the facts 132
 Other convictions and antecedents 132
 Psychiatric difficulties or impaired intelligence 133
 Effect on the victim 133
 Parity and totality 134
 Age 134
 The last run-through before the plea 134
 The plea 135
 Appeal 136

13 Appeals 137
 General 137
 Creature of statute 138
 Preparation 138
 Case stated 139
 Analysis 140
 Drafting 141
 Facts already found 142
 Fresh evidence 143

	Practice	143
	In court	144
	Watch and listen	145
	Precedent	145
	Summary	146

14	Legal writing	147
	Introduction	147
	Preparation	148
	Use the positive and the active voice	148
	Short sentences	149
	Simple words	149
	Dependent clauses and participial phrases	150
	Digraphs	151
	The subjunctive	151
	Personal pronouns and prepositions	152
	Gender neutrality	153
	The gerund	154
	Use words correctly	154
	Plurals	156
	Verbs	156
	Numbers	157
	Comparatives	158
	Politeness	159
	Pleonasm	159
	Other languages	160
	Padding	160
	Overworked metaphors	161
	Sayings	161
	Authorised reports	161
	The start	162
	Quotations	163
	Summary	164

15	Etiquette and ethics	165
	Introduction	165
	Parties and witnesses	165
	Before court	165
	In court before your case is heard	166
	During your case	166
	After the case	167

| *Index* | | 168 |

Foreword

The best advocates are great artists. In this short book I have referred to what some of these advocates have done. My aim is to pass on their lessons. The best advocates have an out-and-out knowledge of all the technical rules. That is their starting point. There are no short cuts. They commit the rules to memory so they can be put to use at a moment's notice.

The best advocates are in tune with courts and fact-finders. They know the law and the court's practice. How they put their skills to use depends on their preparation and their judgment as the case runs. I have written down what many of them have done. But it is not dogma. In every generation there are classy advocates who find some new way of cross-examining, or addressing or doing all those little but important things that are called for in a trial.

Advocacy is a little like the language that is its medium. It is in a constant state of change. The excellent advocates of the past found new means of winning cases. Immerse yourself in their lessons but treat it as a study of history. It is now your task to find your own new ways. We all depend on you to keep the flame of justice burning bright.

Chapter 1

The nature of advocacy

The essence of advocacy

[1000] Advocacy is winning cases. Nothing more and nothing less. It consists in persuading a court to do what you want. The court may have serious misgivings, but the good advocate gives it no choice.

[1005] Victory depends on the sort of case and its strength. Can a plaintiff recover more than the payment into court? Is the contract valid and binding? On a murder charge, can you get a verdict of manslaughter?

[1010] Advocacy is important in a wider setting. As McHugh J said, "Advocacy in the courts is a unique profession. Advocates play an indispensable part in the administration of justice."[1]

[1015] Court work involves the advocate in all sorts of duties. You must do everything legal to win your client's case. You must keep up to date with the law in your field of practice.[2] You must not mislead the court.[3] You must not cross-examine falsely or lead evidence that you know to be untrue. Your private life does not have to be totally without blemish, but of course you must never commit a crime. Honourable does not mean virtuous.[4]

The qualities of advocacy

[1020] Advocacy is a craft. Like every craft it can be learned. The techniques have to be acquired, practised and constantly honed.

---

[1] *D'Orta-Ekenaika v Victoria Legal Aid* (2005) 223 CLR 1 at 38 [104] per McHugh J.

[2] *Copeland v Smith* [2000] 1 WLR 1371; [2000] 1 All ER 457 (CA) per Brooke LJ at 1375; 462. This duty has become very much easier with legislation and decisions of courts now on the internet.

[3] *Clyne v NSW Bar Association* (1960) 104 CLR 186 is a cautionary tale.

[4] David Ross QC "Lawyers' misbehaviour in court and out" (2006) 30 Crim LJ 170–180.

The competent advocate can employ these techniques, but the good advocate is a master of them and moves beyond the craftsmanship that you need in any court appearance. The advocate practising at the higher level of advocacy is an artist with what seems like an easy command of all the know-how. Such an artist does the simple things with supreme style. The master plays the scale better than the pupil.

[1025] Advocacy is played out in a setting that makes it quite different from any other specialty. First, it is done in public. People watch and they judge. Second, every case is different. Not even the newcomer will find the same issues and aspects in every case. Each case has to be custom built. The good advocate will treat every case as the most important ever. It will be prepared and conducted as if it is the last and the one on which the advocate's reputation hangs – as it does. There will be a different approach to each witness. The strategy is prepared to the finest degree, but the good advocate will watch the witness constantly, be ready to adapt the plan and be alert for the need to improvise. It will look effortless.

The qualities of an advocate

[1030] The basic quality an advocate needs is the wish to be an advocate. You must love and need the court work. How many disciplines are there where you can write a script and play a leading part? But you must be able to survive its demands.

> And first, has he a healthy frame, capable of enduring long-continued exertion of mind and body, the confinement of the study, the excitement of practice, the crowded court by day, the vigil of thought by night? Can he subsist with a sleep of five hours? Can he, without dyspepsia, endure irregular meals – hasty eatings and long fastings? If he is not blessed by Nature with the vigorous constitution that will bear *all* this, and more, let him not dream of entering into the arena of Advocacy.[5]

And you must do more than just survive. You must embrace it, love it, live for it. Every old advocate will tell you that the best and worst times of life have been inside a courtroom, from euphoria to misery. The most you can hope for is to do the best professional job. The result is not within your power.

---

[5] Edward W Cox, *The Advocate*, London 1852 p. 10.

[1035] Good physique is not a necessity. Advocates are tall, short, fat, thin, good looking, plain. No doubt the good looking advocate has some attraction, but being well-favoured is probably the least of the qualities an advocate needs. An unhappy physique or unusual looks are never a handicap to one who has the necessary attributes.

[1040] To be a good advocate in court you will need the following qualities:

1. **Voice** You will sound good. Your voice will be well modulated and you will talk slowly. Quality is more important than volume.

2. **Words** You will have a good command of words. When questioning a witness you will use simple language that everyone can understand. Your submissions to the judge will be of the same cast. You will be able to express complex propositions simply without being superficial or simplistic. Your talk will have clarity at least, and often eloquence.

3. **Order** Your submissions and dealings with witnesses will be well ordered and logical. The detailed preparation will be apparent.

4. **Courage** Court work is civilised warfare, and as an advocate you are the champion of the client. Tenacity will be evident. You will not relinquish a central position without a fight. You will be polite but firm and never be belligerent. You want to win. You are not afraid to be silent. Less talk often has more eloquence.

5. **Presence** Every good advocate seems to have a presence. It probably derives from confidence. Many advocates battle nerves before court. You would never know it because the fear falls away when the case starts for the day.

6. **Observation** You will be watching the witness and the judge intently. You will rarely make a note – all the noting must have been done long before.

7. **Wit** You will be quick-witted. If you have a sense of humour you will never use it for its own sake. An advocate with this quality will use humour sparingly and to help win the case. You will never crack jokes.

8. **Emotions** You have a good knowledge of human affairs and of human nature. You will not be afraid to use emotions to advance your client's cause.

9. **Law and evidence** You will know the statute law that applies to the case and the earlier relevant decisions of courts. The rules of evidence seem second nature.

10. **Honesty** Your word is your bond. You never take permanent offence at anything said by your opponent in court or out of it, except for perfidy.

[1045] A good advocate will also possess the qualities of wisdom and judgment. These qualities are often employed in ways that could never be discerned by an observer in court. It is impossible for an onlooker to know what argument the good counsel has decided not to put, what evidence was not called, what issues were omitted from cross-examination. In the running of the case the good counsel will have the intuition to touch on a subject and then perhaps leave it alone. Some of those hard judgments are made in preparation and some are made in the instant. Clarence Darrow, the revered American advocate, said:

> The trying of cases in courts calls for an acute intelligence, the capacity for instantaneous thought and for deciding what to do in the twinkling of an eye.[6]

Cases won on admissible evidence

[1050] In an adversary system the judge's role is to hold the balance between the contending parties without taking part in their disputations.[7] The judge will generally be polite.[8] A trial or hearing is not a pursuit of truth, not even in a criminal case.[9]

[1055] Cases are won on evidence accepted by the court. There is a difference between facts and evidence. Evidence on an issue might never be before a court and thus can never be proved.[10] It is your role to use your best endeavours to have the evidence in your own case admitted, and the evidence in your opponent's case excluded.

---

[6] Clarence Darrow, *The Story Of My Life*, Watts & Co, London, 1932, p. 429.

[7] *Doggett v The Queen* (2001) 208 CLR 343 at 346 [1] per Gleeson CJ; *Robinson v The Queen* (2006) 162 A Crim R 88 at 127 [140] (NSW CCA).

[8] *R v Hircock* [1970] 1 QB 67 at 72 per Lord Widgery LJ.

[9] *Whitehorn v The Queen* (1983) 152 CLR 657 per Dawson J at 682.

[10] There are many cases where facts were not admitted as evidence. See, for example, *R v Sargent* [2003] 1 AC 347; *R v Kirk* [2000] 1 WLR 567; *R v Smith* [1992] 2 SCR 915; *De Jesus v The Queen* (1986) 61 ALJR 1.

[1060] A few examples illustrate the point. Documents may be available to prove a defence but they cannot be obtained. A witness may refuse to give evidence on the ground of self-incrimination. In a contract case the limitation period may have expired. In a bigamy case the prosecution might not be able to provide the strict proof of the earlier marriage.[11] A confession might be excluded because of improprieties by the police,[12] or because it was not recorded by an audio machine.[13] An accused may say that the confession is true, and it can still properly be excluded.[14]

[1065] Thus there may be facts that can never be proved because they can never be put in a legally admissible form. It is your duty to object to your opponent's evidence which should not or cannot be admitted and which does not advance your own case.

[1070] Evidence may be given on which the fact-finder places no reliance. It may come from a witness who has been effectively cross-examined. The witness could be quite disreputable, but in this case may be telling the truth.

[1075] Many cases win or lose themselves because the evidence and the law that is applied are all one way. In these cases advocacy is rather like an exercise in damage control, for damage control is part of the art of advocacy.[15] But a good advocate will win a difficult case. A poor advocate will lose a case that should be won.

How and what to learn

[1080] There is no quick way to learn the skills of advocacy. There is probably no true starting point. One approach is to watch the advocates in the superior courts, particularly in cases where there are witnesses. You will learn how to start and stop a witness and how to direct a witness from one topic to another. This handling of the witnesses rarely appears in the reports of cases or in the books on advocacy. There are special reasons for learning how to guide a

---

[11] The earlier marriage could not be proved in *R v Umanski* [1961] VR 242 (CCA).

[12] For example, lies by police in *R v Anderson* (1991) 1 NTLR 149; 105 FLR 25; 57 A Crim R 143.

[13] For example, the unrecorded alleged admissions by Mr Coates in *Nicholls v The Queen* (2005) 219 CLR 196. See also the earlier case of *Pollard v The Queen* (1992) 176 CLR 177.

[14] This was the accused's evidence on the *voir dire* in *R v Amad* [1962] VR 545 at 549.

[15] *R v Birks* (1990) 19 NSWLR 677 (CCA) at 685 per Gleeson CJ.

witness in this way. The witness is not a lawyer. The witness will not know what evidence is relevant and what evidence is admissible.

[1085] Watch how the good advocate does this so easily:

> Can I just stop you there for a moment . . .

> Thank you for that. May I now ask you about . . .

And to avoid inadmissible hearsay:

> I don't want you to tell us what was said, but did you then speak to Mr Black?

See how the experts do it. Then try it on your friends in ordinary conversation and find out what works for you.

[1090] Watch the examination and the cross-examination of a witness. You may never be able to discern why a witness was asked about a particular subject, or why not. That is because you have not seen the brief of either advocate, and you have not done the preparation and made the necessary fine judgments. You will, however, learn some techniques on how to handle witnesses of different sorts. Then go away and recall how it was done, and work out how you could do it. You will be surprised at the profit of this reflection.

[1095] There is no limit to what a new advocate can learn from watching senior advocates. Even in the appellate courts you can see the different styles and skills in addressing the bench. In these courts the detail of the argument may be hard to follow. All the evidence and the submissions are in writing and filed with the court well before the hearing. The facts are a given. Spoken submissions are designed to advance the advocate's position and reduce the opponent's. But watch the performance. See how these counsel handle the bench. Judge the proficiency and effect. Appeal advocacy at its best is a refined technique. You will spend more time watching appeals when you are called upon to argue one.[16]

[1100] Be cautious about the advocacy you see in the lowest courts. There is a huge range in quality. Some of the old timers are magnificent. A few have been in practice for 30 years, but with the experience of one year repeated 30 times. Some of the younger ones show a good deal of style. There are newcomers still learning the

---

[16] We deal with appeals in Chapter 13.

skills. Check to make sure that what you see and hear in those courts are not the errors that seem to be passed on from one generation of lawyers to the next.

[1105] Read the advocacy books. Keep your eye out for the reports of cases where the questions and answers are quoted with or without approval. Few of the biographies of prominent advocates quote the questioning of a witness except for some stunning remark or curt exchange.

[1110] When I was a young advocate I was often told that it was necessary to develop my own style. I distinctly recall not being able to understand what the advice meant. Should I ask questions in a way nobody else did? Should I try to be different in court from anyone I had seen and admired? I started to put this advice to the test. In the lower courts where I first appeared I tried different styles at different times. Slowly I must have found a style that suited me. You will too. The reason for finding your own style is because the art of advocacy has few, if any, absolute rules. Advocacy is highly individual. What proves effective for one advocate will be ineffective for another.[17] Find a style that works for you.

Good habits

[1115] Knowledge is never wasted in an advocate. It is no burden and can never be stolen. But some knowledge is of more immediate importance. It is worth developing a habit of acquiring particular forms of knowledge. Every good advocate will tell you that learning never stops.

[1120] The following are some of the more important habits.

1. **Law** Keep up to date with decided cases, the authorities. Often enough a superior court will make a decision that will strike you as important. Make a note of it. Soon after I began as an advocate I started taking note of cases under their most obvious subjects and keeping the notes in a loose-leaf folder. It became an alphabetical index of topics. Others have different ways of noting, but all advocates do it. We have to. We would find it too

---

[17] *R v White* (1997) 32 OR (3d) 722 at 745 (Ontario CA). Cited with approval in *Nudd v The Queen* (2006) 80 ALJR 614 at [74] per Kirby J.

hard to absorb a case and try to find the law on the subject from scratch, even with internet resources.

2. **Evidence** You must be thoroughly familiar with the rules of evidence. Evidence consists of the rules and principles that govern admissibility. The rules of evidence are often exclusionary by preventing the proof of some issues. Obvious examples are hearsay, improperly gained confessions, and all manner of documentary evidence.

3. **Rules of procedure** For the young advocate the rules and formalities can be quite intimidating. Has the case come to the right court in the right way? And in court, when do you stand and sit? How do you announce your appearance? What is the procedure for examining witnesses? In what situations can you lose the right of last address?

4. **Court propriety** Stand when spoken to by the judge, be respectful in word and demeanour, and be silent when a witness is taking an oath or affirmation. There is a list of do's and don'ts in the last chapter.

5. **Ethics** These rules have been developed by the profession and occasionally by judges when an advocate makes a serious mistake. You will have to learn them. Nearly all of the ethical problems are likely to arise during the first five years of practice. Again, see the last chapter.

6. **Logic** Logic crops up in court more often than you would expect. One example is the so-called "bootstraps" argument, where the fact to be proved assumes the existence of that fact.[18] Another good example is the wrong argument on DNA evidence. A profile might be shared by a party and only 10 other people in a population of 10 million. Is the probability that the DNA belongs to the party 1 in 10, or 1 in 10 million? Or is it 11 in 10 million? The solution is complex and can only be solved in a given case by reading what experts write about it[19] and what judges say.[20]

7. **Language** Practise speaking simply and slowly. Give up the phrases that mean little: "in relation to", "in terms of", "with

---

[18] *R (Jackson) v Attorney-General* [2006] 1 AC 262 at 288 [48] per Lord Nicholls; *Ahern v The Queen* (1988) 165 CLR 87 at 95.

[19] Such as Kirsten Edwards, "Ten things about DNA contamination that lawyers should know" (2005) 28 Crim LJ 71–93.

[20] For example, *R v Doheny and Adams* [1997] 1 Cr App R 369 at 372–375; *R v JCG* (2001) 127 A Crim R 493 at 508 [79]ff; *R v Karger* (2002) 83 SASR 135.

regard to", "in respect of". Practise the short question that contains only one issue. Try to do what the best advocates do by speaking concisely and accurately.

8. **Politeness** Good advocates are polite in court. They conduct themselves with dignity and courtesy. The primary reason is respect for the court,[21] but the best advocates find that politeness gives their court work a very keen edge. Follow their example.

9. **Watch the bench** When you are in court watch the bench. You may have a plan about the order of your submissions. If the bench interrupts you to ask you a question about something you had planned to speak about later, change your plan. Answer the question.

Duties of the advocate

[1125] These are the duties of an advocate:

1. If you are free you have a duty to accept every case within your area of practice where a reasonable fee is offered. That duty is sometimes referred to as the "cab rank" rule.[22] The metaphor is that the advocate is like a taxi, which must accept anyone prepared to pay the fare.

2. You have no right to refuse to defend in a criminal case, for example, when you believe your client is guilty. There are good reasons for that. Counsel's belief is not relevant.[23] The judgment of guilt or non-guilt is the province of the fact-finder alone. An experienced advocate finds it quite easy not to form a decided opinion, except, of course, in calculating the reaction of the fact-finder to certain pieces of evidence. "How can you represent someone you know to be guilty?" is the question you often hear. The answer would be: "How would I know? I wasn't there. Even if I were there I couldn't have seen from all angles at once, or have seen inside people's minds."

3. You must do your best.

---

[21] " . . . in honour of the Law behind the Judge, and in honour of the People behind the Law." From Alan Paton in *Cry, The Beloved Country* quoted by Callaway JA in *Magistrates' Court v Murphy* [1997] 2 VR 186 at 216.

[22] *D'Orta-Ekenaika v Victoria Legal Aid* (2005) 223 CLR 1 at [17], [27], [142] and [377]; *Harley v McDonald* [1999] 3 NZLR 545 at 567 [62]; *Arthur JS Hall v Simons* [2002] 1 AC 615 at 686 per Lord Hoffman.

[23] *R v McFadden* (1975) 62 Cr App R 187 at 193–194.

> Every counsel has a duty to his client fearlessly to raise every issue, advance every argument, and ask every question, however distasteful, which he thinks will help his client's case.[24]

4. The advocate is not a mouthpiece. You must exercise independent judgment. You cannot be an instrument of fraud, or be a party to misleading the court. No evidence can be led which you know or believe to be false. Nor can there be such a suggestion to a witness, for that amounts to the same thing. If the client charged with a crime tells you he was at the scene but only as an onlooker, you must not suggest to a witness that he was not there. If the instructions change and he tells you that he was not at the scene at all, you will not judge the truth of the instructions. But if he goes on to say that he was at the scene but that he will give sworn evidence that he was not at the scene, then you must withdraw from the case. That is not judging the instructions, but the two versions are contradictory and one of them must be false. If it is any comfort, the need to withdraw because of changed instructions happens so rarely that many advocates will pass a professional lifetime without ever seeing it happen.

5. You must keep up to date with the law in your area of practice.[25]

6. Be polite to all in court.[26]

7. You must never protract a case unduly.[27]

Perfection is not possible

[1130] An advocate is a human being. So are fact-finders. In the nature of things perfection is not possible in either. "Counsel of perfection" has theological origins. It does not derive from any advocate. The highest level to which any advocate can aspire is excellence. Even that standard is elusive. The best cross-examinations and final addresses are in reflection after the case is over. Even the best counsel is never fully satisfied.

---

[24] *Rondel v Worsley* [1969] 1 AC 191 at 227 per Lord Reid.

[25] Etiquette and ethics are summed up in the last chapter.

[26] The worst example of impoliteness many of us have known is by trial counsel in *R v McIntyre* (2000) 111 A Crim R 211 (NSW CCA). It is a cautionary tale. Hulme J, with whom the other judges agreed, said (at 214 [15]): "It is by a factor of very many, worse than anything I have experienced or heard about in my career."

[27] An example of a one-day case protracted to 27 days is *DPP v Sarosi* (2000) 110 A Crim R 376 at 378 [3]–[4] (Vic, Harper J).

Chapter 2

Preparation

General

[2000] You occasionally hear of an advocate who never prepares a case but can win it in court through sheer brilliance. If such advocates exist outside film and television they are out of my class, and out of the class of every advocate I know.

[2005] It is not easy to put down principles of preparation that can be applied to all cases. Every case is unique and must be custom built. Each has its own special aspects, its own idiosyncrasies. The preparation for every case will be slightly or substantially different from any other.

[2010] The main purposes of preparation are to develop a concept of the case, and to work out what you want to do and how you can do it. You should also be able to put your hand on any given document at a moment's notice. While you are preparing you will assemble all the necessary law: precedential, statutory and evidential. Find all of the procedural rules and practices that apply. All these things will work together. Each is essential.

[2015] Preparation can be fearfully demanding. Most cases are won on your effort between 10 pm and 2 am. It is solitary work.[1]

The court

[2020] At some stage you ought to visit the court in which you expect to appear. Look at the judges and listen to them. Try to analyse the style of each. It should not surprise you that not every judicial officer is the same. In common with all humans, each has some quality different from another.

---

[1] Failure to prepare is quite improper: *Putti v Simpson* (1975) 6 ALR 47 (NT, Muirhead J).

[2025] If you have prepared written submissions, one judge will have read and absorbed them. Another would prefer to leave reading until the hearing starts. I have known judges who refuse to read anything before a hearing because they say that they want to keep an open mind.[2]

[2030] Intellectual processes differ. One may be taken with the strict letter of the law. Another may want to make more use of discretion based on experience of ordinary affairs. In the hearing, one may enjoy debate, while another may remain silent until announcing the decision.

[2035] In short, get to know the court in which you expect to appear.[3]

Case concept

[2040] The primary purpose of preparation is to develop a concept of the case. In a trial with witnesses the concept is to work out how you want the evidence to be by the time the case is finished. The evidence will then attract the proper law as you have determined. The combination of evidence and law will gain the result you seek.

[2045] The concept of an appeal is different. Chapter 13 deals with appeals.

[2050] As your preparation in a witness case advances, so will your case concept become more refined. I have heard that some advocates write their final address before the case begins. I have never known any who do, but the principle is correct. You must develop an accurate scheme of the submissions you want to put at the end of the case. Most witness cases turn on one main issue of fact, and a lot of evidence may bear on that issue. If a case does turn on that one main issue, the first part of the preparation should be directed to isolating that issue.

[2055] In most witness cases there can often be side issues. Is a witness telling the truth? Did the witness say something different to

---

[2] David Ross QC, "A good judge" (2005) 26 Aust Bar Rev 102–109. At 103 [5] "I have appeared before judges who prepared nothing, claiming the need for an open mind. I suspect that the real reason was laziness . . . A good judge will bring to the bench the qualities which are shown by good counsel: painstaking preparation and perseverance throughout."

[3] Kirby J, "Ten Rules of Appellate Advocacy" (1995) 69 ALJ 964, had as his first rule "get to know your court". The same principle applies in every court case, not just appeals.

someone else? Did the simple witness sign the ticket without reading its detail? These side issues come and go in a case. Usually you can plan them. But some surprise even the most able advocate, who will know that every so often you have to expect the unexpected.

Never mark a document

[2060] A word of warning: never mark a document that you may have to produce to the court or to a witness. All advocates have seen a witness, when cross-examined, say something inconsistent with a statement in a document held by counsel. The moment arrives for the production of the statement. Counsel says "I'm sorry, I don't have a clean copy", meaning that it has been marked in some way. A hunt is conducted for a clean copy. By the time it is produced the moment is lost. The witness will have recovered some composure. At worst, a clean copy cannot be found. What is marked on the statement is some fatuous comment like "Nonsense!" Sometimes counsel has scribbled instructions in the margin of an opponent's witness statement. Don't do it. There are other better methods of making notes. One obvious method is to put the documents in a loose-leaf folder and insert your own notes on a separate sheet. A more ungainly method that I have seen is for the whole of the brief to be photocopied; counsel marks one of them and the other is kept pristine. Whatever system you devise, don't mark the papers.

Document assembly

[2065] Sometimes an advocate does not have all of the papers. What the papers should contain will vary in different courts and whether it is a civil case, a criminal case or an appeal. Make an index of what you have, and what you should have.

Indexing the case

[2070] In a case involving a number of witnesses, you can compile an index of witnesses to give you an overview. It will help you understand the case. The index may be set out as follows:

Witness	Page	Remarks
ABBOTT, Alice May	91–97	Present at fight b/w dec & another. No i/d of acc.
BROWN, Bruce	62–65	S/C. Photos of scene.
CANT, Clyde	22–23	Ambulance. Victim to hospital.
DRIVER, Denis	102–109	Sgt. Interview with acc: denies involvement.

An index like this will help you get a good picture of events as seen through the eyes of the different witnesses. It will also provide a ready reference during the trial if the name or significance of a witness escapes you. It is easy to compile such a list in alphabetical order on even a basic computer.

[2075] Next make a similar index of the exhibits. The exhibits of the plaintiff or of the prosecution are generally identified by letters, and defence exhibits by numbers. Judges may vary the identification system based on the nature of the case and the exhibits. The index may be set out as follows:

Exhibit No.	Description	Witness	Page
A	Photographs of scene	Const. Brown	62–65
B	Hospital report	Emery	111

The provenance of an exhibit must be demonstrated; that is, its origins must be established. The exhibit produced must be the same or identical, meaning that the exhibit should not have been changed, mixed, contaminated or tampered with on the way.[4]

[2080] Then make a chronological index of events. You need to list the events, great and small, that you expect will be important. This last index should list the evidence that bears on each event and may also include the people connected with the events.

[2085] Choose a method of presentation for these indexes that suits you. You may prefer handwritten notes in folders, or you may wish to use the tools on your computer to aid you in compiling and updating the indexes as the case progresses.

[2090] You then need to work out, in your case, how to prove, reinforce and corroborate the evidence relating to each event, and how to stop your opponent from undermining your evidence or your witnesses. For your opponent's case, you must work out how to prevent or diminish or contradict the evidence relating to each event, or diminish the credibility of the witnesses who give the evidence.

[2095] Your index of events and related evidence contains the essence of how you will run the case. Review the index each day. It will ultimately form an important guide to your final address.

---

[4] For the best evidence rule, see *Butera v DPP* (Vic) (1987) 164 CLR 180 at 194–195 per Dawson J.

Charts, diagrams and drawings

[2100] The case may call for a chart. Complicated financial trans-actions are often set out this way. Where the chart proves to be accurate, judges will often allow it to be tendered as an exhibit.[5]

[2105] Diagrams can be useful in all manner of ways. You may want to draw a diagram to show on a single page how an exhibit passed from hand to hand. Some cases involve a number of parties and witnesses doing different things at different times. Many advocates will make a diagram to help understand the evidence. The diagram will show how each witness claims to have seen the incident in question. One advocate I know is proficient at drawing. In one case he drew what looked like a comic strip representing the observations of one of the witnesses. He did another for the next witness. In the end the drawings showed what each witness said. He put the cartoon strips on one page. The differences in the accounts of each witness were striking and easy to see.

[2110] Not many advocates have that talent for drawing. But I know some who produce a similar result by manipulating drawn figures, and photocopying them. The purpose of all this is to gain an under-standing of what a witness will say, and how it differs from the testimony of another witness.

Photo albums

[2115] Many cases involve photographs. In a civil case for damages for personal injuries, the photographs may be of the instrument that hurt the plaintiff, such as a car or a machine, together with its surrounds. In a criminal case, police photographers go to the scene of the crime and they photograph the scene and the exhibits. The photographs come to the advocate in a booklet, accompanied by a statement from the photographers describing what each photo represents.

[2120] Many advocates undo the booklet and insert the pho-tographs in an album. They copy the photographer's statement and put each description under its relevant photograph. It is quite a quick process. At the end you have an album whose contents you can turn to quickly.

---

[5] *Butera v DPP* (Vic) (1987) 164 CLR 180 at 190.

[2125] There are two advantages in this procedure. First, you get a good idea of what the photos represent. You can look at them under a magnifying glass easily and work out their forensic importance, and the importance of what was not photographed. Second, when you are in court you can turn to the photos easily and know which is a photograph of what. If you do not mount the photos in this way you will be slower in court, for you will need to look at each photograph and then find its description in the statement.

Additional materials

[2130] You may need any of the following to complete your picture of the case:

1. **Documents** These may be obtained by discovery or by subpoena.
2. **Statements of witnesses** Every statement should be in writing and signed if possible. The statement is often called a proof and the taking of the statement is proofing. There is no property in witnesses.[6] Your people can approach anyone to be a witness, even someone who is due to be a witness for your opponent. It is sometimes wise to tape-record the conversation.
3. **Contemporary newspaper reports** Occasionally the newspapers report something different from the case as it comes to you. You may discover the identity of a witness whose evidence could help, or an early statement from a witness that differs from the one you have.
4. **Previous statements of your opponent's witnesses** These may include diaries, notes, and from the police a running sheet of the investigation.
5. **Call records** The police and other emergency organisations keep a recording of emergency telephone calls. Telephone companies keep a record of incoming and outgoing calls for every number.
6. **Medical reports** There may be medical reports on the plaintiff, the victim or even a witness. If a witness for your opponent has been in hospital, the medical staff will often keep notes not only of health and treatment but also of the cause of the injury and the patient's description of the person responsible.

---

[6] *Harmony Shipping Co v Saudi Europe Line Ltd* [1979] 1 WLR 1380 sub nom *Harmony Shipping Co v Davis* [1979] 1 All ER 177 (CA); *R v Ward* (1981) 3 A Crim R 171 (NSW CCA); *R v King* [1983] 1 WLR 411; 1 All ER 929; 77 Cr App R 1.

7. **Opinion evidence** You may need to obtain expert advice on opinion evidence to be called by your opponent, or on some other matter. For proposed opinion evidence for either party, immerse yourself in the specialist literature on the subject.

8. **Background of witnesses (credit)** Write to the (Chief) Commissioner of Police and the Director of Public Prosecutions to obtain the convictions of a witness and information adverse to the credit of that witness.[7]

9. **Exhibits** Examine your exhibits and theirs. Be old fashioned. Look at them under a magnifying glass.

10. **View the scene** Go to the scene, to the *locus in quo*. Make sure that you visit at the hour and day of the week when the events occurred. You may get no profit from it at all. You can't tell until you go. If it is an identification case you may find the lighting poor. Trace the paths of the witnesses. You may discover that they could not have done what they claim. All good advocates do this. They crawl under houses to count the stumps. They drive streets measuring times and distances. They pace out distances against the clock. They make notes all the time. At the very least you will be properly equipped for questioning the witnesses.

[2135] In a civil case there may be a number of steps to take. Do you need an injunction? How will the property be preserved? How do you arrange for the taking of samples? Do you need security for costs?

[2140] Preparation can sometimes be exciting but usually it seems to be a thankless and lonely task. In the early stages at least it can seem like trudging along a dry creek bed. You can never guess when a nugget of gold will appear. No trudge, no gold.

Three examples

[2145] Carson QC defended the Marquess of Queensberry in a criminal libel suit brought by Oscar Wilde. The case has been written about extensively. At the end of Carson's cross-examination of Wilde, the action was withdrawn. The prodigious preparation was obvious. Assiduous detective work by Queensberry resulted in a large dossier of young men who had been familiars of Wilde: names, dates and places were itemised, together with a background

---

[7] *R v Lewis-Hamilton* [1998] 1 VR 630 at 634–635.

on each young man. Carson seems to have read all of Wilde's works. No detail was too small.

[2150] Richard Muir prosecuted Dr Crippen for the murder of his wife by poisoning. His notes for the case were found and published.[8] They are an example to us all.

[2155] Chester Porter was junior counsel to Jack Shand KC in the 1951 Royal Commission into the conviction of Frederick Lincoln McDermott. In 1947 Mr McDermott was convicted of a murder which had happened more than 10 years before. His appeal against conviction was refused by the High Court.[9] The appeal had turned on whether the accused's equivocal confession was properly admitted in evidence. But a Royal Commission was appointed because of concern about the rightness of the conviction. The murderer had driven a car to the scene and the tyre tracks were fresh. The police measured them at the time. Chester Porter tracked down the ancient model of car similar to Mr McDermott's. It was a 1926 Essex Tourer. He measured the tyre tracks. They did not match the tracks at the scene. The Royal Commission found that the conviction was wrong and Mr McDermott was released. Chester Porter was then 25 years old.[10]

Requirements for litigation

[2160] For a matter to be capable of being litigated, it will normally involve four elements:

1. Rights or duties, powers or obligations
2. Of a person who is capable of suing
3. Against a person capable of being sued
4. In a court having power to hear the action.

Elements and evidence

[2165] Write down the elements of the cause of action or of the charge. Can the whole action be stopped, for example, because the limitation period has run out, or because of abuse of process

---

[8] Louis Blom-Cooper ed, *The Law As Literature*, The Bodley Head, London, 1961, pp. 14–33. See also the commentary on the notes by JH Phillips J "Practical Advocacy" (1988) 62 ALJ 627–629.

[9] *McDermott v The King* (1948) 76 CLR 501.

[10] Chester Porter, *Walking On Water: A Life in the Law*, Random House, Sydney, 2003, p. 45.

or prejudicial delay? If not, what is the evidence bearing on each element? Are there issues additional to the elements? To be admissible, any piece of evidence must normally be relevant to an issue.[11] Yet "behind these ultimate issues there will often be many issues relevant to facts in issue".[12] Examine the evidence for your case and the evidence you expect your opponent to lead. Decide whether you can object to any of your opponent's evidence.

[2170] The grounds for objection will usually be:

1. The evidence is not relevant to an issue.
2. The law forbids the evidence, for example, because of public interest immunity.
3. The evidence is not admissible, for example, an involuntary confession.
4. The evidence should be excluded, for example, because a confession was obtained by police improprieties.
5. The witnesses might have colluded.[13]

[2175] Then consider whether you need to make pre-trial submissions. You may need a *voir dire* before evidence can be excluded. Do you need a *Basha* inquiry?[14]

[2180] Look at your index of evidence again. Look at the facts in issue and the facts relevant to the facts in issue. Sometimes the difference between credit and an issue disappears to vanishing point, as Sir Rupert Cross said.[15] Not only that, side issues come and go in a trial: can the prior inconsistent statement be proved, or is the witness telling a downright lie or varnishing the truth, or omitting something which the witness thinks is not relevant? However, the essence of the case will usually turn on one or two issues. Find them.

---

[11] *Smith v The Queen* (2001) 206 CLR 650 at 653–654 [6]–[7].

[12] *Smith v The Queen* at 654 [7].

[13] *Hoch v The Queen* (1988) 165 CLR 292.

[14] Pre-trial arguments on the papers alone are submissions. A *voir dire* is when one side asks the judicial officer sitting alone to hear evidence in order to decide the competence of a witness; or to rule on the admission of other evidence e.g. *MacPherson v The Queen* (1981) 147 CLR 512 at 520. A *Basha* inquiry is having a dry-run in cross-examination of a witness who did not give evidence at committal: *R v Basha* (1989) 39 A Crim R 337; *R v Sandford* (1994) 37 NSWLR 172. See below Chapter 10 [10080]–[10090].

[15] Approved *R v Funderburk* [1990] 1 WLR 587 at 598; 90 Cr App 466 at 475–476; *R v Chandu Nagrecha* [1997] 2 Cr App R 401 at 406; *Nicholls v The Queen* (2005) 219 CLR 196 at 263 [172] per Gummow and Callinan JJ; at 298 [287] per Hayne and Heydon JJ.

Preparing cross-examination

[2185] Most advocates make extensive notes in preparation for cross-examination. Rarely will they write out a question. That will only happen if the question is almost certain to be asked, it must be asked precisely and the exact formulation would be hard to remember. Those three conditions will rarely occur.

[2190] As you work through the evidence of each witness you will discover that you might not have to cross-examine many at all. So much the better. But the evidence of each successive witness will cause you to return to your notes on the earlier witnesses. A case is not just a succession of witnesses. It is a whole, a complete entity. Treat it that way, conscious of the state you want the evidence to be in when the evidence is concluded. Look again to your concept of the case and make sure that your cross-examination of each witness advances your concept.

[2195] For court you will probably summarise these extensive notes. The summary will just be intended as a reminder. The reminder will usually contain:

1. The topics on which you expect to cross-examine.
2. A reference to any prior statement of the witness. The reminder will have a page reference so you can produce the clean document straight away if necessary.
3. A reference to the evidence or statements of other people on those topics, again with page references.
4. Credit matters: is the witness believable?
5. *Browne v Dunn* matters: what evidence of the witness do you expect to contradict by other evidence or in your submissions?[16]

These reminder notes of only a page or two will be near you during your cross-examination. Of course you will tailor your questions according to the evidence-in-chief. Expect not to have to refer to them more than by the occasional glance. Notes are not a script.

Child witnesses

[2200] The preparation to cross-examine a child witness takes a little imagination, for the cross-examination itself takes a good degree of delicacy. A child often gives evidence in a criminal case either as a victim or as an eyewitness. It sometimes happens that those

---

[16] *Browne v Dunn* (1893) 6 R 67. See below Chapter 5 [5075]–[5100].

who have spoken to the child have so infected the evidence as to make it worthless.[17] You will need to find all those who have spoken to the child about the events, especially relatives. You can also get the notes from a government department that may have dealt with the child and from the police who spoke to the child before video interview. The child may have been coached. Those notes can be obtained by subpoena. Repetition of a question to the child implies that the first answer was not satisfactory. Recommendations of proper procedures are set out in the Cleveland Report carried out in England.[18] If the child's evidence is admissible, the next decision is whether the child can give sworn evidence. That depends at least on age and knowledge of right and wrong, and other factors such as competence.[19]

Admissions

[2205] There may be an issue of fact which you know will be proved by your opponent but you don't want the fact-finder to hear the evidence. The most usual example is the proof of death. The fact of death is rarely an issue. It can be the basis of a civil case, for example, by a widow or by beneficiaries. It may be a criminal charge over a person's death: murder, manslaughter, causing a death by dangerous driving and so on. The last thing you want is for a jury to hear a distraught relative give evidence of identifying a deceased loved one. A typical admission is in writing and signed by defence counsel. The document is often tendered. Here is an example:

> The person depicted in photograph 1 is Noel John Williams. On 4 September 1987 he died at Essendon. He was 50 years of age at the time of his death.[20]

[2210] You will need to take care with an admission. An admission once made ceases to be a fact in issue. It is normally just read to the fact-finder, and often the document containing the admission is tendered as an exhibit. The fact, once admitted, ceases to be one on which there can be evidence-in-chief or cross-examination.[21]

---

[17] *R v Warren* (1994) 72 A Crim R 74.

[18] Referred to in *G v DPP* [1998] QB 919 at 926.

[19] *Revesz v The Queen* (1996) 88 A Crim R 253.

[20] *R v Hughes* (Supreme Court of Victoria) 17 July 1990.

[21] Sometimes it is possible to withdraw an admission, at least in a civil case: *H Clark (Doncaster) Ltd v Wilkinson* [1965] Ch 694, unless it is too late: *Langdale v Danby* [1982] 1 WLR 1123; [1982] 3 All ER 129.

An admission will have the following qualities:

1. It must be an admission of fact. There can be no admission of law.[22]
2. It is a formal procedure.[23]
3. In a criminal case it must not be unfair to an accused.[24]
4. It should be in writing.[25]

During the trial

[2215] Every night during the case, continue your preparation in the following ways:

1. Index the day's transcript. Where the evidence is on computer disc, there is still no relief. One character might variously be referred to as Mr Smith, that red-headed man, or the bloke they all called Bluey. An event might have a similar difference of description. Note the evidence and the page and line numbers. If there are errors in the transcript, bring those to the attention of the judge so that they can be corrected. Do not mark the transcript for you may have to show one of those pages to a later witness.
2. Prepare for tomorrow. It might be refining a cross-examination because of today's evidence, or using today's evidence to mount a legal argument.
3. Make notes of your final address. Start or continue to prepare your final address. Be sure to write down important non-evidential matters, such as the demeanour of a witness or the time taken to answer a question.
4. Note grounds of appeal. Note and draft any ground of appeal that has arisen today. You may never need them. But it is so easy to do each night while it is fresh in your mind. Drafting the grounds of appeal after the case has finished is a fearfully daunting task, and you cannot avoid the fear that you have left out something important.

Luck

[2220] Painstaking preparation means that luck will run your way.

[22] *R v Stokes and Difford* (1990) 51 A Crim R 25 (NSW CCA) at 32 per Hunt J.
[23] *Byrne v Godfree* (1997) 96 A Crim R 197 at 202 (WA, Walsh J).
[24] *R v Balchin* (1974) 9 SASR 64 at 67 (CCA).
[25] *R v Birks* (1990) 19 NSWLR 677 at 702 per Lusher AJ.

Chapter 3

Witnesses and questions

Witnesses

Witness statements

[3000] All witnesses will give some indication of their evidence before the case is heard. In a civil case a plaintiff will go to a lawyer who will note down what the plaintiff says. This is the client giving instructions. The defendant will provide a list of witnesses who may be spoken to first by an insurance investigator. The investigator will prepare a written report on the people interviewed and what was said. The choice of witnesses will then be refined, and the main ones will see the defendant's lawyer who will of course note carefully what is said.

[3005] In a criminal case it is the police who take statements from the witnesses. The police themselves make statements as part of their duties.

[3010] Expert witnesses make statements as a matter of course. Depending on the area of expertise, an expert may be asked to examine an injured plaintiff, or a firearm, or any number of items to check for blood or DNA and so on. Invariably the expert witness will report the findings in writing.

[3015] In a civil case you can ascertain the essence of your opponent's case from the pre-trial documents. Generally each side gives notice of the evidence of any expert witness it intends to call. In a criminal case a prosecutor has a duty to give witness statements to the defence.

Choosing which witnesses to call

[3020] It is very rare that an advocate will call a witness without knowing the nature of the evidence the witness can give. In most cases the advocate will have close at hand the statement of the witness or at least a lawyer's note outlining a conversation with the witness. On these documents and on their analysis, the advocate will first determine whether the evidence is relevant, and if so, whether the witness is reliable. You must not call a witness whose evidence you know to be false, whatever the jurisdiction. This proposition derives from an advocate's overriding duty not to mislead the court.[1] In a civil case each advocate can choose which witnesses to call if any.

[3025] In a civil case each side calls the witnesses it chooses. In a criminal case a prosecutor must call all witnesses necessary to the unfolding of the narrative.[2] The advocate for an accused can choose which witnesses to call, if any.

Civilian witnesses

[3030] Civilian witnesses vary from the frightened to the self-possessed to the garrulous. In preparation there is a temptation, which is hard to resist, to conclude that one witness will be largely truthful and another the reverse. We often tend to think that the witness who advances our version of the case is a truthful witness. With very rare exceptions, demeanour is a poor guide to truth and accuracy. As Chester Porter QC said:

> The best witness I ever saw, whose demeanour was 100% perfect, was Australia's top con man.[3]

[3035] Occasionally a witness will reply with a question.

> Did I cross the road? Of course I did. Why shouldn't I?
> Yes, I crossed the road. Wouldn't you have done the same thing?
> Yes. What would you have done?

The best way to treat these questions is to regard them as rhetorical. Make no answer. In fact ethically you are not allowed to answer. Above all avoid the pompous rejoinder: "I'm asking the questions in this court!"

[3040] Nearly all witnesses are polite and confine their evidence to the questions they are asked. Occasionally witnesses will get miffed

---

[1] The etiquette and ethics are summarised in the last chapter.
[2] *Seneviratne v The King* [1936] 3 All ER 36 (PC) at 49 per Lord Roche; *Whitehorn v The Queen* (1983) 152 CLR 657 at 674 per Dawson J.
[3] Chester Porter QC *Bar News* (NSW) Spring 1999, p. 20.

if they feel they are being prevented from giving all of the evidence they want to give. This will often be true because a witness might not be aware of what evidence is relevant and what is admissible. Imagine that you have done your best to guide a witness away from a piece of evidence that should not be given. Sometimes you will then hear a response of this sort: "Why are you stopping me from telling the truth?"

[3045] Usually the judge or magistrate will speak to the witness about keeping the evidence to the point of the question. What is often more useful, particularly in a jury case, is for you to give a brief explanation. Say something to the following effect and with politeness:

> I must explain to you, Mrs Green, that court cases run on rules. There are things you can say and things you can't say. If I leave something important out, (name or describe your opponent) will ask you or the judge will correct me. Do you understand?

I have found that this seems to work fairly well.

Practised witnesses

[3050] Some witnesses give evidence in court so often that it seems almost part of their ordinary functions. Many police officers fall into this class. Their training includes practising giving evidence in court. Each police officer must keep a diary of essential events and for every case must make a formal statement. The police witness will have read and memorised the statement before giving evidence. Nevertheless like all of us they do make mistakes. The statement (and the evidence) may refer to events the witness believes occurred but might not have seen. The evidence of one police witness may conflict with another, or with a civilian witness. The witness might have acted improperly. Some police are allowed to give opinion evidence because they are considered to be experts. These include firearms examiners, fingerprint experts and document examiners and those from the police forensic science laboratory. Many of these experts regard themselves as scientists who happen also to be police.

[3055] There are expert witnesses who give evidence so often that they are skilful witnesses. These witnesses often hold official positions in quasi-government organisations. Commonly you will encounter pathologists and biologists. You will have cases involving engineers, geologists, anthropologists, accountants, town planners – the number of experts and variety of disciplines never fail to surprise.

Witnesses who make a mistake

[3060] Identification of a person, a voice or an object is fraught with uncertainty. An honest and impressive witness can be completely mistaken. Court cases are full of such examples.

[3065] Police officers take written statements from many people. The procedure is as follows. The officer will often be quite well acquainted with most of the evidence in the case. The proposed witness comes to the police station and they talk. The officer then prepares a statement based on that conversation. The witness signs the statement, having first been told that the statement and signature are just a formality. The witness may not have been told of the possibility of being called as a prosecution witness.

[3070] Often a statement taken by the police will contain mistakes. I leave out for the moment the few cases where the police have deliberately intimidated a witness. Those whose statements contain mistakes generally fall into two classes. The first is the person who doesn't read the statement properly and the statement does not quite accord with what was said. Before the person is called as a witness, police may say that departure from the statement may result in a charge of perjury. The second is the person who does not tell the whole truth in the statement. The witness may be personally embarrassed or have someone to protect.

[3075] Insurance investigators take statements from witnesses in a manner similar to the procedure followed by the police. They point out the duties to provide information under the terms of the insurance policy.

Witnesses who lie

[3080] It is not easy to come to the conclusion that a person would tell a deliberate lie in the witness box. Yet your preparation might drive you to that conclusion, and your client or independent people may confirm your suspicions. A witness who lies usually has a purpose to serve in giving false evidence. A prisoner who claims that the accused confessed to him is one example.[4] Another is an accomplice.[5] The evidence of the accomplice is often very persuasive because of the accomplice's inside knowledge of the crime.[6]

Hostile witnesses

[3085] With leave from the bench, a hostile witness can be cross-examined. A hostile witness is one who gives false evidence, or deliberately withholds evidence, due to an unwillingness to tell the truth at the instance of the party calling the witness, or for the advancement of justice.[7] The *Uniform Evidence Acts* provide for cross-examination of an "unfavourable witness" with the leave of the court.[8]

Questions
Use simple English

[3090] Use simple English in your questions. The reasons are obvious. First, the witness has to understand the question. Second, the fact-finder has to understand both question and answer. Simple English is the form in current use. By that I do not mean that your questions will be in slang, although you should listen for colloquialisms. What we might think of as slang could be the ordinary expression of a witness. Here is an example from a Supreme Court criminal trial. A prosecution witness was giving evidence-in-chief about the accused speaking to him.

> What did he say? — He told me to fuck off.
> And did you? — Yes.

The jury would have understood the expression. It would have sounded wholly contrived for the prosecutor to have asked: "What did you understand him to mean when he said that?"

---

[4] See *Pollitt v The Queen* (1992) 174 CLR 558, especially at 614–615 per McHugh J; *Benedetto v The Queen* [2003] 1 WLR 1545; 2 Cr App R 390 at [32]–[35] (PC).

[5] *Vetrovec v The Queen* [1982] 1 SCR 811 at 823; *Jenkins v The Queen* (2004) 79 ALJR 252 at 256 [25].

[6] *R v Ncanana* [1948] 4 SALR 399 at 405; *R v Clarke* (2001) 123 A Crim R 506 (NSW CCA) at 547 [67] per Heydon JA.

[7] *R v Hutchinson* (1990) 53 SASR 587 (CCA) per King CJ at 592.

[8] *Evidence Act 1995* (Cth); *Evidence Act 1995* (NSW); *Evidence Act 2001* (Tas) s.38. See also *R v Le* (2002) 54 NSWLR 474 (CCA).

[3095] All language in current use is in a constant state of change. What is simple English in one generation will not be nearly so simple in the next. In 1922, Cussen J suggested that after you show a document to a witness, the question would then be to the following effect:

> Having looked at the document, do you still adhere to your previous statement?[9]

These days we might prefer to ask two questions on the issue, such as:

> Have you looked at the document?
> Do you still stick to what you said?[10]

[3100] Simple English means that you do not use Latin words or phrases. Avoid *ergo*, *ipso facto* or *sub judice*. Do not use lawyer's jargon either. We sometimes hear an advocate use the tortured expression: "I would have thought that that might very well be the case." This prolixity simply means "possibly". Another common example is: "I would have thought that the duration of the case would take some little time." It is far better to give your best estimate ("About two weeks, Your Honour").

[3105] The use of simple English is particularly important when questioning experts. Some experts may feel the need to give evidence in technical or specialised English. Simple English may lack the precision they feel is needed to convey the information. They may want to use the technical or specialist terms that are common in their field. As part of your preparation you will have studied and understood the specialist terminology. However, it is essential that you still use simple words when asking your questions, for if the expert agrees with the question, the evidence will be clearer for the fact-finder.

Never "the accused"
[3110] When defending in a criminal trial never refer to the person for whom you act as "the accused". It is impolite[11] and it can depersonalise the case. Never say "my client" or "the plaintiff". To my ear it connotes a distasteful commercialism. Always use the correct

---

[9] *R v Orton* [1922] VLR 469 at 470.
[10] More detail is given in Chapter 8 [8050].
[11] *R v Williams* [2001] 1 Qd R 212 at 218 [18]–[19].

title of the person for whom you act: Professor, Dr, Mr, Mrs, Miss or Ms. Sometimes, but not often, it is proper to refer to the person for whom you appear by his or her given name. Aboriginal people often refer to each other only by given name. If it is the polite designation, you should too.[12] Always use names rather than general court designations. It sounds respectful. Take away the name, and you forget the identity.

One issue to each question

[3115] Each question should contain a single issue. More than one issue in a question reveals the sloppy thinking of the questioner. Worse than that, when confronted with such a question, the witness may not be able to answer. In some cases, the witness may answer but the court is left in doubt as to which part of the question is being answered. A very cool-headed witness may even ask which part of the question to answer. So take care to keep your questions as simple and precise as possible. Practise until it becomes second nature. In general, the shorter the question the better:

> Are you taking anti-depressants? — No.
> Were you taking anti-depressants? — I was.
> What years were you taking anti-depressants? — I couldn't tell you.
> For years? — (witness answers).[13]

Brevity brings clarity. The best questions are those that take up only a line or two on the transcript.[14]

Avoid negative questions

[3120] Shun negative questions, and be especially careful to avoid the double and multiple negative.

> You didn't cross the road, isn't that so?

> It would be incorrect to say that you were not alone, would it not?

---

[12] I often referred to Quentin Tipungwuti as Quentin because I was assured that it was proper. For the traditional folk of Central Australia, the polite designation is usually the skin name, such as Tjakamarra (or whatever the skin name might be).

[13] Examination-in-chief by Andrew Haesler (later Haesler SC): *R v Fowler* (2003) 151 A Crim R 166 at 200.

[14] The single exception to one issue per question may be when you allege that a witness invented the evidence. See Chapter 6 [6135].

Few witnesses could answer questions like these. Negative questions violate the primary rule that the witness and the fact-finder should be able to understand the question. Be vigilant. Every advocate has fallen into the negative question trap at some time or other.

No padding

[3125] Your questions should be as precise and unambiguous as possible. For that reason avoid using questions that contain the phrases "in relation to", "in terms of", "with reference to", "in respect of", "with regard to". They lack exactness. These phrases are properly referred to as padding.[15] In turn, the answers to questions containing padding will lack the precision you are looking for. The less precise the question, the less useful the answer. You can replace these phrases with simple prepositions such as "about", "on", "of". The best way to avoid padding in your questions is to abandon it in your ordinary speech. Then have a look in the law reports at some of the questions that use padding, and redraft them using the simple prepositions.[16]

Never argue with a witness

[3130] Above all, you must never argue with a witness. Challenge the evidence, assail the character or credit of the witness, but never argue. Here is an example of what not to do. The witness was a cantankerous prisoner, but that was no excuse for the cross-examiner's truculence.

> Is that all? What about, leaving aside the women that you have murdered, have you assaulted many women? — Let's go. Name them.
> No, Mr Brazel? — No, I haven't.
> How many women have you assaulted? — I just told you, I haven't.
> None? — Not to my recollection.
> Is that a truthful answer? — That is a truthful answer, yes. Now that you can put that accusation, can you name one? You can't can you.
> You're a very slow learner, Mr Brazel, aren't you? — Approximately as slow as you . . .[17]

---

[15] Strunk and White, *The Elements of Style* 4th ed, 2000, Longman, New York, p. 50.

[16] There are many examples of padding in questions such as in *Grey v The Queen* (2001) 75 ALJR 1708; 184 ALR 593 at [11]–[12]. Worse still is padding in judgments and in legislation. See Chapter 14.

[17] *R v Johnson* (2001) 126 A Crim R 395 at 413 (Vic CA).

Timing

[3135] Delicacy of timing is a valuable quality in asking questions of a witness. These days the atmosphere of the court is more matter-of-fact than in any former time. The florid flourish has had its day. But when actors deliver their lines, timing is crucial, and the principle is no different for the advocate who wants a question or answer to be given added weight. As an advocate at the height of your powers you are alive to the atmosphere of the court and have a commanding presence. When you are on your feet, the court is silent and in complete attention. You will speak to be heard, and usually no louder. You will make subtle changes in pitch and volume to enhance the effect you want. Timing is one of your weapons. Hastings KC summed it up years ago:

> There can be no doubt that real and legitimate dramatic effect can be obtained both in the voicing and the timing of a question.[18]

Leading questions

[3140] A leading question cannot generally be asked during examination-in-chief except on formal matters or on matters not in dispute. Leading questions can be asked in cross-examination, although these can be curtailed.[19]

A leading question means a question asked of a witness that:

1. directly or indirectly suggests a particular answer to the question; or
2. assumes the existence of a fact the existence of which is in dispute in the proceedings and as to the existence of which the witness has not given evidence before the question is asked.[20]

[3145] Leading questions take different forms. Here are some of them:

> You walked across the road, did you?
> Didn't you walk across the road?
> You walked across the road, didn't you?

---

[18] Patrick Hastings, *Cases in Court*, 1949, William Heinemann, London, p. 288.
[19] *Mooney v James* [1949] VLR 22 (Barry J); *R v Coventry* (1997) 7 Tas R 199 at 202 (Slicer J); Mildren J "Redressing the Imbalance Against Aboriginals in the Criminal Justice System" (1997) 21 Crim LJ 7 at 15–16; *Evidence Act 1995* (Cth); *Evidence Act 1995* (NSW); *Evidence Act 2001* (Tas) s.42.
[20] *Evidence Act 1995* (Cth); *Evidence Act 1995* (NSW); *Evidence Act 2001* (Tas).

It's true that you walked across the road, isn't it? (or some similar forceful form).

[3150] A short simple question works perfectly when you are guiding a witness through a series of actions to establish what came next:

Cross the road?
Walked across?

Leading questions to avoid

[3155] There are some forms of leading questions that you should never use:

I put it to you (that you crossed the road).
I suggest to you (that you crossed the road).

[3160] Although these forms of leading question have passed through generations of advocates, you should never use them. Never. One judge described such a question as "ineffectual".[21] There are three reasons why these forms of questions are wrong. First, they are not in everyday speech. Second, they are not questions, even if you add at the end: "What do you say to that?" They are only an invitation to argument. Third, you deprive yourself of a question best designed to fit the case and the witness. A formula question is never as good as one that is carefully designed to fit the evidence. It lacks style.

[3165] There are other ineffectual questions that you sometimes hear: "My client will say (that you crossed the road)", and "Are you trying to persuade the magistrate/judge/jury (that you crossed the road)?" Worse than ineffectual, questions like these do not address any issue in the case.

[3170] Lord Hewart CJ railed against these forms of questions so many years ago.

One often hears questions put to witnesses by counsel which are really in the nature of an invitation to argument. One hears, for instance, such questions as this: "I suggest to you that . . ." or "Is your evidence to be taken as suggesting that . . ." If the witness were a prudent person he would say . . . "What you suggest is no business

---

[21] *R v Teys* (2001) 161 FLR 44; 119 A Crim R 398 at 53; 408 [54] (ACT, Miles CJ).

of mine. I am not here to make suggestions at all. What are the conclusions to be drawn from my answers is not for me ..." *What is wanted from the witness is answers to questions of fact.* One even hears questions such as: "Do you ask the jury to believe ..." [my emphasis].

His Lordship then disparaged that last form.[22]

Do not comment on an answer

[3175] One bad habit of many advocates is commenting on an answer. You often hear, or read on transcript "OK" and then the next question starts. Other such comments are "Right" and sometimes, "I see". A worse comment is repeating an adverse answer. Here are two examples. The first contains straight comments:

> You said that on the morning the police came that you couldn't remember what you'd done with the heroin? — At first I couldn't, no.
> Right. And you said that Ian was handcuffed to the stair, do you remember that? — That was later on in the morning, yes.
> Okay. Did you see a video. . . .[23]

The second example is the cross-examination of a child victim of a sexual offence. Note how the cross-examiner gets adverse answers and, worse still, repeats them:

> The [appellant] never touched your rude part? — He did.
> He did? He never showed you any dirty magazines? — He did.
> He did? Do you remember that? — Yes.
> When did that happen? — When he tried to hump me.
> He tried to hump you?[24]

[3180] All advocates make a comment at some time or another. What we should never avoid is the intended comment. When a witness, such as an expert, gives a careful and considered answer, an advocate will sometimes say, "Thank you". The good advocate only gives that sort of remark if the atmosphere of the court calls for it. These comments can never be planned but the advocate with a flair for atmosphere and timing will use a comment instinctively, and to great effect.

---

[22] *R v Baldwin* [1925] All ER Rep at 404–405; 18 Cr App R 175 at 178–179.

[23] *R v Le* (2002) 130 A Crim R 44 at 54 [16] (NSW CCA).

[24] *R v DAH* (2004) 150 A Crim R 14 (SA CCA) at 23 [45].

When a witness needs an interpreter

[3185] Some witnesses need an interpreter. Some accused are questioned by police through an interpreter. Interpreters vary enormously in skill and experience. Some do not have sufficient knowledge of one language or the other.[25] The difficulties in questioning a witness through an interpreter are more extensive than just the problems with language. It is hard to see if the question is causing the witness to pause before answering and whether a non-responsive answer is caused by failure to understand the question properly. If the witness is your opponent's, it may be a good idea to have your own interpreter there to make sure that the interpretation is correct.

[3190] There are certain skills called for when questioning a witness through an interpreter. The questions must be short, sharp and clear. Look at the witness and not at the interpreter. Above all direct your questions to the witness and not to the interpreter (ask "What did you do?" not "What did she do?"). Question the witness in the same way you would question a witness whose language you share.[26]

Watching the witness and listening

[3195] See how every good advocate watches the witness and listens to the answers. This technique applies to all questioning, whether examination-in-chief, cross-examination or re-examination. Every question follows from what the witness has already said.

[3200] John Scopes was charged with teaching evolution. In Tennessee in 1925 that was an offence. William Jennings Bryan prosecuted and Clarence Darrow defended. Darrow was not allowed to call evolutionists to give evidence, so he called Bryan as a bible expert. In this extract you can see Darrow watching and listening intently:

> You believe the story of the flood to be a literal interpretation? — Yes sir.
> When was that flood? — I would not attempt to fix the date . . .
> But what do you think that the Bible itself says? Don't you know how it was arrived at? — I never made a calculation.

---

[25] For an example, see *R v Lars and Others* (1994) 73 A Crim R 91 at 116 (NSW CCA).

[26] An excellent example is the cross-examination by M J Lee in *Chong & Toh v R* (1989) 40 A Crim R 22 at 41.

A calculation from what? — I could not say.

From the generations of man? — I would not want to say that.

What do you think? — I do not think about things I don't think about.

Do you think about things you do think about? — Well, sometimes.
(*Laughter*) [27]

Demeanour: even temper and politeness

[3205] Court cases are formal public occasions. For that reason, if for no other, you must always be polite and at least give the appearance of even temper. A court case will not always go as you plan it. Some cases seem to be doomed from the start and are little more than an exercise in damage control. Politeness and even temper are effortless when the case is going well. But when the case is not going well, or the tension is high, the strain involved in maintaining courtesy is more difficult. But politeness has its own rewards. It gives forceful advocacy a keen edge and it keeps the fact-finder on side.

[3210] Courtesy in court means that you never bicker with your opponent. You do not want the fact-finder to think that the contest is not about the evidence but about which advocate is going to survive the personal slanging march. Don't distract the bench from the evidence, which must always be central. There is a further disadvantage to bickering. A judge could tell a jury not to be distracted by the ill manners at the Bar table, and chastise counsel publicly.[28] That is the last thing you want. I knew one counsel who regularly played the man. He lost some cases probably because the jury resented the personal attacks on his opponent.

[3215] Good demeanour does not mean that you forsake firmness or even indignation when they are called for. Your words must be measured and deliberately chosen to advance your case. They must never reveal a lack of control.

---

[27] Arthur Weinberg, ed., *Attorney for the Damned*, 1957, Simon and Schuster, New York, pp. 198–199. A shortened version is in Irving Stone, *Clarence Darrow for the Defense*, 1941, Doubleday & Co, New York, p. 516.

[28] *Beevis v Dawson* [1957] 1 QB 195 at 201 per Singleton LJ.

Chapter 4

Examination-in-chief

Proof of the case

[4000] Every case, civil or criminal, can succeed only if it is supported by convincing evidence. Otherwise the case is doomed. The support for the case is by evidence-in-chief. When an advocate calls a witness who gives evidence in answer to the advocate's questions, that evidence is called examination-in-chief.

[4005] The primary art of the advocate is to conduct examination-in-chief in its most persuasive form. The most cogent form of evidence-in-chief is where the story of the witness seems to emerge at the witness's own pace. The advocate seems to play little part, which is as it should be. The seemingly simple story belies the skill of the good advocate. The evidence will be in the right order and it will be complete. If there is no objection from the defence, that is because the advocate has guided the witness away from evidence that is not admissible. Even though the witness is telling the story, the advocate has the witness under control, with only the slightest hint of intrusion here and there. Evidence-in-chief wins most cases.

Defence witnesses

[4010] Once the case is made out, the defence can call witnesses. Sometimes the evidence of defence witnesses is a complete denial of the claim, such as in civil cases where the contract on which the plaintiff relies is a forgery, or in criminal cases, where there is an alibi. More often the defence evidence is intended to cast a different light on the claim. (Yes, the defendant did borrow the money but subsequently repaid it.) In a prosecution the defence may be intended to show accident, self-defence or provocation.

[4015] All the same principles of leading evidence-in-chief apply to witnesses called by the defence.

[4020] Defence advocates are sometimes reluctant to call evidence because of the risk of losing the right of reply. Court practice sets an order of final addresses. The plaintiff or prosecutor addresses first and the defence second. But when the defence leads evidence, the usual order of addresses may be reversed. Advocates place great store on the right to be the last to address the fact-finder, and for that reason will hold on to the right of reply if possible.

Level of detail

[4025] The amount of detail in evidence-in-chief will depend on the need to explain to the fact-finder the aspects of the case that could not be common knowledge. For example, where a sexual offence is alleged to have taken place inside a house, the evidence-in-chief may have to explain the layout of the house. Where the evidence is of identification in a street at night, a description of the street and the position of lighting will be called for. Where the operation of a machine is in issue, some detail of that machine may need to be given about how it works and perhaps an explanation of some of the technical terms or jargon. For example, the fact-finder may not be familiar with the language used by computer experts. Computer graphics, and the photos, plans and diagrams will need to be explained. These are the sorts of things that the advocate will call on a witness to clarify in detail in evidence-in-chief.

No leading questions

[4030] Leading questions are not permitted in evidence-in-chief. The only exceptions are on formal matters, or evidence on a subject that is not in dispute.[1]

[4035] There is the further exception of permitting a denial of a central allegation. Sexual assault cases provide a good example of this exception. In evidence-in-chief the victim can be asked: "Did you consent?" That form of question is either not leading or simply directing the attention of the witness to an issue in the case.[2]

[4040] The advocate can direct a witness to an issue. So, again in a sexual case, no fault was found in the following question asked in evidence-in-chief:

---

[1] See also *Uniform Evidence Acts* section 37.
[2] *Saunders v The Queen* (1985) 15 A Crim R 115 (WA CCA); *R v Shaw* [1996] 1 Qd R 641; 78 A Crim R 150 (CA).

Did you do anything to try and stop him?[3]

Some books contain long lists of exceptions. In general they are just examples of directing a witness to a particular topic.

[4045] It is usually not leading to give the witness a choice, particularly of extremes.

Was the car going fast or slow?

You can often find a question that is even less subject to doubt.

How fast was the car going? OR What was the speed of the car?

The Bolster rule

[4050] Evidence is admissible if it bears on the issues in the case or if the evidence is about facts relevant to the facts in issue. But in examination-in-chief, credit is not an issue. Thus in examination-in-chief you are not allowed to ask questions simply to bolster the credit of a party or of a witness. That evidence is just not admissible. As McHugh J said:

> The rule stipulates that evidence is not admissible if it merely bolsters the credit of a party or witness, whether the evidence is sought to be led in evidence-in-chief or cross-examination of another witness or in re-examination of the party or witness attacked.[4]

Watching the witness and listening

[4055] You should always have to hand the statement or proof of the witness. If you are not well prepared you will have to concentrate on the proof, with perhaps the occasional glance at the witness. If you do this you run the risk that the fact-finder might conclude that if you are not paying attention to the witness, then why should the fact-finder? Ideally you will have mastered the detail of the evidence that the witness can give. You may wish to make your own précis of the evidence, and you may glance at that from time to time to make sure that nothing is left out. Above all, you should watch the witness closely. There should be eye contact between witness and

---

[3] *R v Markulesi* (2001) 52 NSWLR 82; 125 A Crim R 186 at 112; 214 [128].
[4] *Palmer v The Queen* (1998) 193 CLR 1 at 22–23 [49] per McHugh J.

advocate. This is the primary method of enabling the witness to give evidence in its most persuasive form. It sets the witness at ease. Both witness and advocate think that the evidence is important, and the fact-finder will too. This is the best way of keeping the witness under control. You should watch the judge and jury out of the corner of your eye, but your attention will seem to be given wholly to the witness.

Setting the witness at ease

[4060] Most civilian witnesses are apprehensive about giving evidence in court. The formality is daunting. All but the most stout-hearted witnesses will quail when standing in the witness box with everyone watching. For your case to have the best chance of success you want the witness to be able to give persuasive evidence-in-chief. It is customary to ask the address and occupation of the witness.[5] Of course you can begin examination-in-chief with:

> Is your full name John Thomas White, do you live at 27 High Street Brighton and are you a computer programmer by occupation?

There can be no objection to these leading questions because they are all on formal matters. What will set the witness at greater ease will be non-leading questions. You can be sure that the witness will get the answers right, and it settles the witness. Just as important, you do not intrude because you don't have to.

> What is your full name? — John Thomas White.
> Where do you live, Mr White? — 27 High Street, Brighton.
> And your occupation? — I'm a computer programmer.

[4065] Most expert witnesses are quite practised at giving evidence. Again, if you do not want to intrude, you might ask:

> Doctor, what is your full name? — James Anthony Grey.
> Your occupation? — I'm a pathologist.
> What are your qualifications, Doctor? — (qualifications given)
> What experience do you have? — (experience given)
> Where do you carry on practice?

---

[5] Address and occupation are, strictly speaking, irrelevant other than "to locate the witness in society": *R v Chen & Ors* (2002) 130 A Crim R 300 at 312 [28] (4) (NSW CCA).

Forms of questions

[4070] The most useful forms of non-leading questions begin with who, what, when, where, why and how. Here is a short example from a case where the plaintiff said she had slipped on the stairs at work and hurt herself. The defendant called the plaintiff's superior. Here is part of the examination-in-chief:

> When you went to work, how did you travel? — I drove the car and parked at the roof car parking.
>
> Did you use the stairs that led from the roof into the building on a regular basis? — Yes, yes.
>
> What sort of shoes did you wear? — They were leather soled, sometimes some had a rubber heel.[6]

[4075] You can also base the question on what the witness has already said. In this example, a complainant was giving evidence-in-chief of sexual assaults. See how the advocate encourages the detail:

> Now after that first time, did anything like this ever happen again? — Yes it did.
>
> How many times? — Every time I went over to use the phone, up until we moved to Johnstown.
>
> And how many times would that have been? — Several.
>
> Do you have any idea how many? — 10 to 20 maybe. Maybe a few more.[7]

[4080] In the next example, the witness had earlier said that she had a conversation with the accused. Note how the advocate combines reliance on the earlier evidence and then the non-leading questions:

> During the course of the conversation that you and the accused had, did he tell you something? — Yes.
>
> What did he say? — First of all I thought he said something along the lines of he lopped his Dad's head off. I thought he said he cut his Dad's head off, basically.
>
> As best you can say, what were the words that he used when he said that to you? — "I lopped my Dad's head off."[8]

---

[6] *Makita (Australia) Pry Ltd v Sprowles* (2001) 52 NSWLR 705 at 728. See also Chapter 7 [7050].

[7] *R v François* [1994] 2 SCR 827 at 850; 91 CCC (3d) 289 at 306.

[8] *R v Martin (No 2)* (1997) 68 SASR 419; 94 A Crim R 357 (CCA) per Doyle CJ at 422–423; 360.

[4085] In an examination-in-chief it might be necessary to ask a witness about going to a particular place. You might ask:

Where did you go?
Why did you go there?
How did you travel?
When did you arrive?
How long did you stay there?

[4090] The questions will be short and expressed in simple English. Simple English is honed with practice. The questions must not be ponderous. Use "After that" instead of "Subsequent to that occurrence". You should never be verbose because questions in this form can sound bombastic. Verbosity and pretentiousness are fundamental flaws in any form of examination.

Stopping and starting a witness

[4095] One of the great skills of a good advocate is the ability to stop and start a witness with politeness. You can observe this skill in every court where a witness is giving evidence. There will be a variety of reasons for stopping a witness. One of them is to avoid inadmissible evidence.

Don't tell us what was said, but did you then speak to Mr Black?

Another is to stop the witness so more detail can be given.

Can I stop you there for a moment, please? — Yes.
You said that you went into the house? — Yes.
Can you describe the layout of the house after you enter the front door?

Another reason for stopping the witness is to avoid irrelevant detail.

[4100] Starting a witness is usually done by directing the witness back to the earlier narrative.

After you left the house, what happened then?
OR You said earlier that you left the house? — Yes.
What happened after that?

[4105] The following example comes from a case where the accused woman is giving evidence-in-chief. The subject is the conversation with her husband. Walsh QC is insistent but very polite.

What happened then? — He wanted a divorce. He started talking straight away that he wanted a divorce and he wanted . . .

If I could just interrupt you, and pardon me for it, it is perhaps easier if you could use his exact words where you can, or to the best of your recollection, and your words back. Could you try and do that for me please? — I'll try.[9]

The right order

[4110] The order of giving evidence-in-chief enables the court to follow the evidence with ease, and to understand it. In general, chronological order is best. Finish each incident or topic with all of its necessary detail before moving to the next. Questioning an eye-witness is a good example. The witness to a traffic accident might be asked questions in this order:

What took you to that place?
Exactly where were you?
What was the state of the traffic?
Did you see the collision?
Where did each car come from?
Will you describe the collision as best you can?
Did you see anything after the collision?

A witness to an armed robbery might be directed through evidence with the following order of questions:

How did you come to be there?
Did you see the victim?
Did you see the accused?
Was the accused carrying anything?
What happened?
What happened to the victim?
Where did the accused go?
For how long did you see the accused?
Did you later identify the robber in the police line-up?
Do you see that person now?

If you ignore the correct order, you may confuse the witness and therefore the court.

---

[9] *Van Den Hoek v The Queen* (1987) 28 A Crim R 424 at 425.

[4115] The order for a medical specialist might be:

> What information did you receive before examination?
> What did you find on examination?
> What is your diagnosis?
> What is your prognosis?

The order for a pathologist might be:

> When were you asked to examine the deceased?
> What information did you have, such as details of previous treatment?
> Who was the person you examined?
> What did you find on examination?
> What was the cause of death?

[4120] Of course you will need to adapt your questions according to the nature of the evidence. Work out in advance the correct order. The ultimate purpose is for examination-in-chief to be clear and persuasive. The evidence should be taken in a commonsense order to make it most easily understood.

Refreshing memory

[4125] Soon after an event occurred, the witness may have written down what happened, although this is quite rare for a civilian witness. These notes can be used to refresh the memory of the witness during evidence-in-chief. Notes made much later cannot be used.

[4130] A civilian witness may have trouble remembering something quite important. That forgetfulness will not be helped by the formality of the courtroom. Guide the witness to that matter as gently as possible. If the witness still cannot remember, pass to the next topic. Gradually the witness will warm to the occasion of speaking about the events, and will probably become more relaxed. Return gently to the forgotten idea. The witness may now remember the incident because it fits as part of the whole episode she has spoken about already.

[4135] Expert witnesses will have made an examination of a person, a machine or some item. During that examination they will take or dictate fairly comprehensive notes. Courts rarely expect expert witnesses to remember all of the detail of their examinations without looking at notes. Experts are allowed almost as a matter of course to refresh their memories from their notes.

[4140] There are other witnesses, such as police officers, who take notes as part of their ordinary duties. Most police will keep a diary and if some important event occurs will make a formal statement as soon as possible. Before giving evidence a police witness will use these notes to bring the events back to mind as much as possible. In most cases police witnesses will be required to exhaust their memories before being allowed to refer to notes. If the witness has notes but no memory of the events, the notes must be produced if called for.[10] The examination-in-chief might be:

> Do you have any trouble recalling these events? — Yes, I do.
> Did you make any notes about the events? — Yes, I did.
> When did you make those notes? — I made a diary entry immediately after, and then I compiled a statement as soon as I got back to the police station.
> At the time when you made that diary entry and the statement, were the events fresh in your memory? — Yes.
> Can you give full evidence of these events without refreshing your memory? — No.
> I seek the leave of the court for the witness to refer to his diary and his statement.

[4145] In the following example, Elizabeth Fullarton SC's careful questioning helped the witness to bring as much as possible back to mind during evidence-in-chief. It comes from *R v Chen, Siregar and Others*.[11]

> After that, did you speak with a person about the derrick? — Yes.
> Do you know the name of that person? — Yes.
> What is his name? — Siregar.
> What did you say to Mr Siregar? — That the boss asked us to lengthen the derrick.
> What, if anything, did he say to you? — Yes, but I don't remember.
> Are you able to recall anything that Mr Siregar said to you after you spoke to him, just yes or no for the moment, please? — He did say something but I forget.
> Do you remember where you were when you spoke to Mr Siregar at this time? — On deck near the derrick.

---

[10] *R v Alexander and Taylor* [1975] VR 741.
[11] *R v Chen and Others* (2002) 130 A Crim R 300 at 356.

Did you say anything else to Mr Siregar after he spoke words to you that
you are unable to recall? — Basically it's about the oxygen, whether
there would be enough oxygen to do the welding.

Do you recall if Mr Siregar said anything to you as you spoke about
oxygen and welding and these matters? — I recall that he said that
there was not enough on board the ship.

Toning down weak points

[4150] During examination-in-chief it is often a good tactic to bring
out any weak points rather than risk a damaging impact in cross-
examination. You will often use this device when an accused is
giving evidence that differs from the account that was given to the
police. Here is an example from a murder case. The victim had
broken into the accused's room carrying a beer bottle and a knife.
The accused picked up a rifle, shot the victim and dragged him back
to the victim's own room.

After that what happened? — After that I went back to the corridor and
picked up the beer bottle and the knife.

What did you do with those? — I walked back into flat 5 and threw the
knife towards the kitchen sink and placed the beer bottle on the side
table near his door.

At one stage you told the police, I think, that you just threw the beer
bottle in? — Yes, Yes. I got it incorrect.[12]

[4155] Leading questions can always be asked with your opponent's
consent. Here is an example of a prosecutor introducing the failure
of his witness to identify the accused. Every question is leading. The
defence advocate would never object.

I think some time after that, on 8 February 1985, you were asked to go
to the police station and then to the Magistrates' Court, is that right?
— I'm not sure of the exact date but, yes I . . .

No, but there was a day, some weeks later, when you did that? — Yes.

You went to the Magistrates' Court, is that right? — Yes.

You looked around but you were unable to see anybody you could
identify as the person who first got into your cab? — That's right.[13]

---

[12] *R v Hughes* (Vic CCA 20 March 1990, unreported).
[13] *Lewis v The Queen* (1987) 88 FLR 104; 29 A Crim R 267 (NT CCA) at 112; 283.

Good character

[4160] Evidence of good character can be relevant in a wide variety of cases. In a defamation case Lord Denning suggested the following form in questions about a party:

> Who are you? [Lord Denning probably meant name and occupation.]
> How long have you known him?
> Have you known him well?
> Have you had an opportunity of observing his conduct?
> What character has he borne during that time for honesty, morality or loyalty (according to the circumstances of the case)?
> As far as you know, does he deserve this character?[14]

[4165] In a criminal case, evidence of good character of the person charged bears on the improbability of guilt[15] and the likelihood that the person charged is truthful.[16] In *R v Rowton*[17] the court said that this evidence of good character must be confined to evidence of good reputation. The case has been followed in the highest courts. Depending on the circumstances of the case, the questions might be as follows:

> Do you know the accused?
> How long have you known her?
> Do you know those who also know her?
> Are you able to speak about her reputation?
> What is her reputation for honesty?

Summary

[4170] In summary, these are my recommendations:

1. Use simple English.
2. Include only one issue per question.
3. Ask questions in the right order.
4. Use non-leading questions. Guide without leading.
5. Keep control. You can stop, redirect and restart a witness without being intrusive.
6. Watch the witness and listen to the answers.

---

[14] *Plato Films Ltd v Speidel* [1961] AC 1090 (HL) at 1139 per Lord Denning.

[15] *Attwood v The Queen* (1960) 102 CLR 353 at 359 (applying *R v Rowton*).

[16] *R v Murphy* (1985) 4 NSWLR 42

[17] *R v Rowton* (1865) Le & Ca 520; 169 ER 1497 (Full Court of Crown Cases Reserved).

7. Be thorough. Obscure terms and slang may need explanation, the layout of rooms or streets may need description.
8. Be prepared to refresh the memory of the witness.
9. Be prepared for a witness to be hostile.
10. Tone down weak points.

Chapter 5

Cross-examination: its qualities

The nature of cross-examination

[5000] Cross-examination is the questioning of an opponent's witness. Some learned judges have described cross-examination as "a potent weapon for probing the credibility and reliability of an accuser's version of events"[1] and "a powerful and valuable weapon for the purpose of testing the veracity of a witness and the accuracy and completeness of his story".[2] Another judge said: "Cross-examination is an art, and the means used to cut down the effect of the evidence of a witness . . . are multifarious."[3] Yet another judge said: "It is the most important part of the advocate's art, because a competent cross-examination is designed to weaken or destroy the opponent's case and to gain support for the client's case."[4]

Is it necessary?

[5005] Planning will show whether it is necessary to cross-examine a witness at all. You will not cross-examine if the witness does your case no harm, and if you cannot get some advantage to your whole case or disadvantage to your opponent's case.

> [I]n cross-examination, every question that does not advance your case injures it. If you do not have a definite object to attain, dismiss the witness without a word. There are no harmless questions here; the most apparently unimportant may bring destruction or victory.[5]

---

[1] *R v NRC* [1999] 3 VR 537 (CA) at 551 [33] per Winneke P.

[2] *Mechanical Inventions v Austin* [1935] AC 346; All ER Rep 22 (HL) at 359 per Viscount Sankey LC approving Lord Hanworth LC in the court below.

[3] *R v Birks* (1990) 19 NSWLR 677 at 686 per Gleeson CJ.

[4] *R v Sharp* [1994] QB 261 at 273 per Stuart-Smith LJ giving the judgment of the Court of Appeal (Cr D).

[5] Edward W Cox, *The Advocate*, 1852, London, p. 433.

[5010] Sometimes you must cross-examine when it is the last thing you want to do. If the witness gives devastating evidence-in-chief, you must do your best to limit the damage.[6] A cross-examination that simply repeats evidence-in-chief is a serious misjudgment.

Main aims

[5015] The main aims of cross-examination are these:

1. To advance your own case.
2. To reduce the evidence-in chief of the witness:
   (a) by destroying the evidence;
   (b) by weakening the evidence;
   (c) by undermining the credit of the witness.
3. To set the evidence of one witness against the evidence of another.

Only ask questions that have these aims.

[5020] In many cases the core of the claim or of the prosecution case is not in issue. The defence may concede the formation of the contract, the injury to the plaintiff or the killing of the victim. You may have a defence that does not call into question the essence of your opponent's case. In the contract case, the defence may be that the contract was performed until further action under the contract became impossible. In the injury case, the defence may argue simply that the injuries are not very serious and the plaintiff has returned to work. In the criminal case, the defence may be accident or self-defence. Most of the evidence giving the basis for these defences will come from cross-examination of your opponent's witnesses.

[5025] It is a rare case where the evidence of a witness will be completely destroyed in cross-examination. When it does happen, usually the witness is proved to be quite wrong on a central issue. Proof is generally by some strong documentary evidence.

[5030] In most cases the plan is to weaken the evidence of a witness. For example, you might be able to show that before giving evidence the witness has said or written something altogether different – a prior inconsistent statement. By weakening the evidence I mean that its effect is reduced to such a degree as to give the fact-finder

---

[6] This happens more often than any advocate wants. An example is *Vesey v Bus Eireann* [2001] 4 IR 192 at 200–201.

grave doubts. When the evidence is circumstantial, the effect will be that damaging inferences cannot be drawn. Perhaps there is another hypothesis that the witness will concede is plausible, or which can later be argued. Your argument will derive its force from the failure of the evidence to prove the hypothesis that forms the basis of your opponent's case.

[5035] Many different matters can undermine the credit of a witness. The witness may have a string of convictions for offences of dishonesty. The eyewitness might not have been wearing glasses. The earwitness might not have heard the conversation at all but have been told about it by someone else. The biologist might not have done the tests – someone else did.

[5040] The final method is to cross-examine one witness in order to undermine the evidence of another. There are some rules about this. The undermining must be on a question of fact. You cannot use the evidence of one witness to attack the credit of another.[7] One witness might say that you can see very little from a particular position. When an eyewitness comes to give evidence of seeing an incident from that position, the fact-finder may have real doubts about the accuracy of the evidence or even its truth.

[5045] These are the main aims or objectives of a cross-examination. The techniques that advocates employ to achieve these aims are set out in the next chapter. It is important to note that there is no single technique for any given aim.

Relevance

[5050] The cross-examination must be relevant to some issue in the case. The primary issues are the elements of the cause of action or of the crime. Cross-examination on the evidence about the elements will be of obvious relevance. Behind these are facts relevant to facts in issue.[8] With one witness it may be the quality of the observation. Another witness may be cross-examined to show that he and his evidence are unworthy of credit.

[5055] A judge has the power to curtail or even stop a cross-examination.[9] The judge will rarely do that because some of the

---

[7] Although one witness can speak of the bias or partiality of another.

[8] *Smith v The Queen* (2001) 206 CLR 650 at 654 [7].

[9] *R v Higgins* (1994) 71 A Crim R 429 at 442 (Vic CCA).

most effective cross-examinations have begun by getting the assent of a witness to a proposition of seeming irrelevance.[10]

[5060] The carefully prepared cross-examination will not be stopped. The most a judge will do is to make sure that the question is relevant and the advocate must be ready to justify its relevance. In *R v Anderson* a sergeant of police was cross-examined to show that he had lied to the accused to obtain a confession. He said it was an "interrogatory lie". That was a lie told to obtain an account from a person he was interviewing. The transcript shows that the questioning went on:

> Counsel: The interrogatory lies, are they a valid method of speaking to people? — I don't know . . .
> Counsel: Is it a technique that you used on occasions other than this one?
> Martin J: Does that help?
> Counsel: Yes. One of the authorities invites you in the exercise of your discretion to determine a public policy question. *Bunning v Cross.*
> Martin J: Yes, all right. (to the witness) What's the answer to that?[11]

[5065] The ramshackle cross-examination that takes a long time because it is clearly ill-prepared, and where there are long pauses while counsel hunts through papers for some document, is the most likely to be stopped.

The rule in *Browne v Dunn*

[5070] Every cross-examination must comply with an important rule of practice. The rule is that you must cross-examine on every material fact in dispute. The rule applies whether the cross-examiner proposes to cross-examine another witness to show that the evidence is in dispute, to call another witness to that effect, or to make final submissions that the evidence should not be accepted.

[5075] The rule in its present form derives from a decision of the House of Lords in *Browne v Dunn*.[12] It is designed to bring fairness to a case so that the parties are given the chance to join issue. It also

---

[10] *Wakeley v The Queen* (1990) 64 ALJR 321 at 324.

[11] *R v Anderson* (1991) 1 NTLR 149; 57 A Crim R 143. Part of the cross-examination is reported but the exchange between Martin J and counsel is not.

[12] (1893) 6 R 67 at 70–71 per Lord Herschell.

affects the weight to be given to evidence of a later witness.[13] When issue has been joined, the evidence of a later disputing witness comes as no surprise. Absence of compliance might lead to the suspicion that the later witness invented the evidence.

[5080] In cross-examination to comply with the rule, you should never use the formula questions "I put it to you" or "I suggest to you". Chapter 3 dealt with the form of such questions and how they must be avoided.[14] True artistry calls for questions to be precisely designed to achieve their purpose. Formula is the absence of mastery and thought.

[5085] Questions that comply with this rule of practice can range from the merest hint to the strongest assertion. Assume in this example that later evidence will show that a witness to a central event crossed the road. The question might be one of the following, depending on the aim of the cross-examiner:

> Is it possible you crossed the road?
> Did you cross the road?
> It's a fact, isn't it, that you crossed the road?

[5090] These are only three possible ways of compliance. The best method will be what the cross-examination of the witness calls for. Here is a straightforward example:

> Did you say to him [i.e. to Lawrence]: "Stefan my husband has been playing round with Helga"? Did you say that to him? — I said nothing like that to Mr Lawrence. I simply said, "Mr Lawrence, I'm looking for my husband."
> Did you say this to Mr Lawrence, "I'm going to give him up to the police unless he gives me my share of the property"? Did you say that? — No. No. I didn't.
> Did you say, "If he sells up and gives me two thirds I will say nothing"? — No, definitely not.[15]

Watch the witness

[5095] When a witness is giving evidence-in-chief, young advocates tend to bury themselves in their notebooks and try to write down

---

[13] *Bulstrode v Trimble* [1970] VR 840 at 846–848 (Newton J); *Allied Pastoral Holdings v FCT* [1983] 1 NSWLR 1 (Hunt J).

[14] See Chapter 3 [3150] and following.

[15] *R v Umanski* [1961] VR 242 at 243.

as much as they can. Then they get to their feet to cross-examine, based on the notes. Experienced advocates take an entirely different approach. They have already planned the case to the finest degree. During examination-in-chief they watch the witness with an attentive eye, except perhaps for a glimpse around the court or to make a brief alteration to their notes for cross-examination. Some chance remark in evidence, some pause in answering, may alter the plan completely. Good advocates may forego the planned cross-examination altogether or decide to cross-examine a witness they had not expected to. Often they will recast the planned cross-examination based on an estimate of the witness.

[5100] Charles Russell QC was always alert in court. He took no notes. His eye was on the witness, but he would glance around, sometimes at the judge, sometimes at the jury or counsel on the other side. In one case his junior was taking notes assiduously. Russell said, "What are you doing?" "Taking a note," was the answer. "What the devil do you mean by saying you are taking a note? Why don't you watch the case?"[16]

[5105] Cross-examination is no different. You should always watch the witness. You must listen carefully to the answers and tailor the rest of your questions based on every answer the witness gives. Young advocates may lack confidence to watch the witness in this way, perhaps due to misgivings about the quality and thoroughness of their preparation. But from the outset you should try to emulate this method of the good advocates. As one venerable silk wrote: "It is better for the cross-examiner to study his witness, after studying his brief, than to act as an unobservant but meticulous recording clerk."[17]

Leading questions

[5110] Leading questions can be asked in cross-examination. However, they should not be asked as a matter of course. A good advocate will mix leading with non-leading questions. The witness who is inclined your way should need few leading questions. A witness of dubious credit may not be asked too many leading questions at

---

[16] R Barry Breen, *The Life of Lord Russell of Killowen*, Thomas Nelson &, London, pp. 102–103.

[17] Sir Robert Menzies, *Afternoon Light*, 1967, Cassell & Co, London, p. 338. Sir Robert was Owen Dixon's only reader. After a stellar career as a junior he took silk in 1929, aged 34. It was later that he took up a full-time political career.

all, for that may arouse the sympathy of the jury for the witness. In nearly all cross-examinations, the good advocate will ask as many non-leading questions as possible. The witness will be under the advocate's control, generally without apparent effort. The form of each question will be designed to fit, and will never cause a slackening of that control.

[5115] Here is an example of defence counsel cross-examining a prosecution witness. The purpose is to undermine the witness's power of observation and identification.

> You were stoned on marijuana that night? — Yes.
> How many joints had you smoked? — I don't know.
> You had drunk alcohol? — Yes.
> Were you drunk? — No.
> How much had you had to drink? — I don't know; two, three, four cans. I didn't count them.
> Any pills? — No.[18]

[5120] The following examples are of non-leading questions by prosecutors in cross-examination. Prosecutors often use non-leading questions to allow an accused to provide more implicating detail. In the first example the defendant was cross-examined about a fishing spot:

> Have you fished that area before? — Yes, I have.
> From when? — Since I was a kid. My old man used to take us there all the time.[19]

In the next example, the accused was cross-examined about forcing his wife to have sex with him:

> Did anything like that ever happen? — I pressured her to have sex, yes.
> When you say pressured her to have sex, what do you mean by that? — Basically, I suppose it could be considered emotional blackmail. Just, stating, what a husband and wife I'd say there should be some form of sexual contact between us.
> How would that, as far as you were concerned, emotionally pressure her into having sex? — She felt guilty and often conceded to my request.
> Did you ever physically force yourself upon her? — It could be looked at that way, yes.

---

[18] *R v Einem* (No 2) (1991) 52 A Crim R 402 at 420.
[19] *Sutton v Derschaw & Ors* (1995) 82 A Crim R 318 at 323 (WA, Heenan J).

In what way could it be looked at like that? — (witness answers)
And what sort of things would you do? — (witness answers).[20]

In the next example, an accused was cross-examined about his evidence that he had stomped on a woman's arm:

What did you do to her arm? — Yeah, I stomped on her arm.
Where was her arm? — Right next to the – like on the side of her.
Which arm was it? — Her right arm.
Why did you do it? — I'm not sure.[21]

In the final example, a prosecutor was cross-examining a defence witness to show partiality. Notice the non-leading questions at the start:

Are you a friend of his? — I'm a colleague and I was his principal.
At the time when the allegations were made? — Yes.
Would you regard yourself as a friend? — I would now.
Would you agree that you are on his side? — Yes, I would.
Your personal view, if you like, is that the allegations aren't true —
    Yes.[22]

Forms of question

[5125] Some advocates caution against asking a question where you don't know the answer. That warning is too comprehensive. Better advice is not to ask a question on a central issue where you cannot anticipate what the witness will say. If part of the skill of cross-examination is keeping control of the witness, you should never ask questions that leave witnesses at large to answer whatever they may. For that reason be very cautious about using questions starting with who, what, when, where, why or how. Wrongly used, such questions hand control to the witness.

[5130] Here is an example of a witness being allowed a free hand. In a criminal case a witness had given evidence at a preliminary hearing, often called a committal. The witness had said in the committal that he was 70 per cent sure that the person he met was the

---

[20] *Case Stated by DPP (No 1 of 1993)* (1993) 66 A Crim R 259 at 283 (SA CCA).
[21] *R v King* (2004) 150 A Crim R 409 at 420 [38]. The cross-examining prosecutor was Eric Balodis.
[22] *R v Kostaras* (No 2) (2003) 86 SASR 541; 143 A Crim R 254 at 550; 263 [31] (CCA).

accused. At trial he said he was completely sure. Identification was a central issue. Consider the following questions by defence counsel:

> Why are you now 100 per cent sure?
> What's changed?
> Why didn't you say that on the last time, that you were really sure that it's him?
> Why is last time different to this time?[23]

As you may imagine, the answers of the witness dismantled the defence. But worse than that, the chance to demonstrate the fallibility of the identification was lost. The trial evidence of identification put the defence in a degree of damage control. What would you do, as good advocate? First, you would have to hand exactly what the witness had said at the preliminary hearing. Second, you would construct the cross-examination so that in your final address you could say that the identification evidence was wrongly improved, which is contrary to all human experience. These are some possible questions:

> Have you given evidence in this case before today?
> Was that in the preliminary hearing?
> That was on (date), wasn't it?
> (The accused) was in that court?
> Were you asked if you could identify him?
> You said you were only 70 per cent sure you could, didn't you?
> (If necessary, take the witness to the precise answer in the transcript.)
> Did you give that answer on your oath?
> Swearing to tell the truth?
> (and if your instructions and the other evidence justifies it . . .)
> And you haven't seen him between then and now, have you?

[5135] The best advocates will often use a non-leading question when they are certain of the answer, or when the answer doesn't matter. As an example of the former, let's say that a sober witness drove to a party, and that some event, which is the subject of the case, happened at the party. All of the witnesses described in their statements who was where in the car. It may suit you to ask non-leading questions. Try these short ones:

> Who was driving? — I was.
> Anyone beside you? — Yes.

---

[23] *Al-Hashimi v The Queen* (2004) 181 FLR 383; 145 A Crim R 186 at 388; 191 [19] (WACCA).

Who? — George.
Anyone in the back seat? (and so on).

[5140] Here is an example from Jack Shand QC. He was cross-examining a police officer about the taking of a statement from a witness who was a friend of the accused. Some time later the police officer told the witness that the accused was charged with murder. The witness said, "I am very sorry I told you so much." Shand had all of the documents. His questions were non-leading because he knew the answers.

You thought that was a genuine kind of remark? — Yes.
Did you ask him to add it to the statement? — No.
Have you made any notes of your conversation with him? — No.[24]

[5145] Non-leading questions can also be asked when the answer does not matter. This occurs when you are trying to turn one falsehood into many, a lie into a litany. Take the following example.[25] Samuel Warren was cross-examining a witness to the signing of a will. In those times, the proof of the authenticity of a will was that the testator signed it and put a wax seal at the bottom, or a wafer. The witness stood to gain from the will. During his cross-examination Warren held up the will with his thumb over the bottom.

I understand you to say that you saw the testator sign this instrument? — I did.
And did you sign it at his request, as subscribing witness? — I did.
Was it sealed with red wax or black wax? — With red wax.
Did you see him seal it with red wax? — I did.
Where was the testator when he signed and sealed this will? — In his bed.
Pray, how long a piece of red wax did he use? — About three inches long.
And who gave the testator this piece of wax? — I did.
Where did you get it? — From the drawer of his desk.
How did he melt that piece of wax? — With a candle.

---

[24] John Wentworth Shand QC's cross-examination of ex-detective-sergeant Phinn, 20 August 1959, in Royal Commission into the conviction of Rupert Max Stuart (K S Inglis, *The Stuart Case*, Melbourne University Press, 1961, reprinted Black Inc, 2002, at p. 130).
[25] The example is from Wellman, *The Art of Cross-Examination*, 4th ed., 1936, Simon & Schuster, New York.

Where did the candle come from? — I got it out of a cupboard in the room.

How long should you say the candle was? — Perhaps four or five inches long.

Do you remember who lit the candle? — I lit it.

What did you light it with? — Why, a match.

Where did you get the match? — On the mantel-shelf in the room.

Now, sir, upon your solemn oath, you saw the testator sign this will – he signed it in his bed – at his request you signed it as a subscribing witness – you saw him seal it – it was with red wax he sealed it – a piece of wax about three inches long – he lit the wax with a piece of candle which you procured from a cupboard – you lit the candle with a match which you found on a mantel-shelf? — I did.

Once more, sir – upon your solemn oath, you did? — I did.

[*Mr Warren takes his thumb from the base of the will.*]

My Lord, you will observe this will is sealed with a wafer!

"Closing the gates" and "tightening the net"

[5150] Advocates sometimes use metaphors to describe techniques of cross-examination. One of them is "closing the gates". Literally, a farmer will close the gates to prevent stock from getting out. As a figure of speech it describes how an advocate cuts off any chance of escape of a witness. The advocate induces the witness to deny every possibility except the one that promotes the cross-examiner's case. The advocate closes the gates one by one.[26]

[5155] In north-east Arnhem Land there was a Yolngu man named Tanka Tanka. He described how a cross-examination carefully demolished the evidence:

I am a fisherman. I heard your cross-examination. You threw a net around that policeman and drew it tight. Then you made a small opening for a fish to come out and you speared it. Then you did it again and again until there were no fish left.[27]

This is tightening the net.

---

[26] An example of "closing the gates" is in Chapter 8 [8090].

[27] Tanka Tanka was in the gallery of a coroner's inquest into a police shooting of a Yolngu man. The part of the inquest he heard was at Galiwinku, Elcho Island, on 19–20 June 1990.

Knowing when to stop and how

[5160] Knowing how and when to stop is as important as knowing how to start. The good advocate plans both. The last thing you want is for your cross-examination to fade away in an inconsequential manner. Plan to finish strongly so the court's last impression of the witness is one that clearly favours your case. The end will affect the atmosphere of the court as much as the start. As one of my colleagues used to say after such a finish to cross-examination, "My bum hit the seat in a shower of sparks."

One question too many

[5165] You occasionally hear that a cross-examination was undone by one question too many.[28] Put this way, it seems as if the misfortune can be known only after the event as if it were unforeseeable. This is not quite correct. The one question too many is usually about the conclusion or the irresistible inference that can already be drawn from the evidence. Do not ask the witness to agree with the conclusion. The question is superfluous. Worse, the witness may disagree with you and give perfectly cogent reasons. So watch and listen, and resist the temptation to deliver the *coup de grâce*. The inference or conclusion will be all the more powerful if the fact-finder is led inescapably to it without your baldly stating it.

[5170] An example of one question too many is asking about an important issue where you don't know and cannot calculate what the answer will be. Don Campbell QC, a prominent Australian personal injury advocate, told this story against himself. He was cross-examining the plaintiff's doctor.

> How would you describe the pain? — Like a red hot iron placed on the sole of the foot.
> What would you know about a hot iron placed on the sole of the foot? — I was a prisoner-of-war in Changi.[29]

---

[28] In *R v Burns* (2003) 137 A Crim R 557 (NSW CCA) Sully J said (at 573 [76]): "It is a truism that a good barrister is always astute to avoid the temptation to ask the one question too many."

[29] Don Campbell QC, speaking to the author in 1971 about a case he had been in a decade or more before. Changi was a Japanese prisoner-of-war camp in Singapore during World War II. The doctor was (Ernest) Edward "Weary" Dunlop, famous for his ministrations to his fellow prisoners. Dr Dunlop was knighted in 1969.

Chapter 6

Cross-examination: method and style

No one correct technique

[6000] There is no one correct method of cross-examination. One advocate may be comfortable with a style that will be hard won by another advocate. But whatever your style, you will use different techniques with different witnesses. You will also use different techniques with the one witness. The nature of the witness and the content of the evidence will give you the clues. Choose the techniques that suit your style and the witness you are cross-examining.

[6005] The only method of cross-examination that can clearly be identified is confrontation. Confrontation means challenging a witness with damaging facts to break down the witness's story. Other methods of cross-examination involve undermining a witness in various ways. Often you will use the evidence of one witness to undermine the evidence of a central witness for the other side who has not yet given evidence. If you have material that contradicts the evidence-in-chief you may prefer to persuade the witness to agree with the contradictory evidence. Advocacy as the art of persuasion often includes persuading a witness.

[6010] Trying to characterise the different techniques is not easy. What may be more valuable is to examine examples from actual cases.

Confrontation

[6015] You can only confront a witness when you have real material to work with. This is armed combat. The material might comprise the statements or evidence of the witness or of other people. That material will be at odds with the evidence-in-chief of the witness. But the converse does not apply. Material that is quite different from the evidence-in-chief will not always be used to confront the witness. Confrontation is a technique not very often used, or if it is, perhaps in one part only of the cross-examination. Make a total confrontation of the witness only when it is necessary to destroy that witness's evidence.

[6020] As is well known, Oscar Wilde brought an action for criminal libel against the Marquess of Queensberry. Carson QC represented the defendant. The cross-examination shows that Carson had an enormous amount of material in his brief and was able to put his hand on any document at any time. Carson had to ruin the witness if Queensberry were to have any chance at all. Carson's opening gambit must have been decided only after Wilde's examination-in chief. This evidence was given in April 1895. Carson began by confronting Wilde's false understatement of his age.

> You stated that your age was thirty-nine. I think you are over forty.
> You were born on 16th October 1854? — I have no wish to pose as being young. I am thirty-nine or forty. You have my certificate and that settles the matter.
> But being born in 1854 makes you more than forty? — Ah! Very well.[1]

[6025] Patrick Hastings KC recounted one of his successes. A crane was unloading boxes of oranges and one of them fell to the pavement. A man was found groaning on the footpath claiming injury. Insurance companies were canvassed. The plaintiff had earlier claimed the same injury with a different cause and the case was settled. Further, the plaintiff and his family had bought derelict houses, and claimed to have renovated them before they had been burnt to the ground. Each had first been insured. Hastings wrote that his opening question was:

> I am going to suggest to you that this case is a deliberate fraud, and that for years past you and your family have lived by making fraudulent claims upon insurance companies.[2]

---

[1] H Montgomery Hyde, *Oscar Wilde*, 1975, Farrar, Straus and Giroux, New York.
[2] Hastings KC, *Cases in Court*, 1949, William Heinemann, London, pp. 13–17. In fact this was a statement rather than a question.

Drawing out every damaging detail

[6030] Evidence may exist that damages the evidence-in-chief of
a witness. The evidence may imply that the witness is of doubtful
memory, observation or truth. The skill is to draw out every damaging detail. If the witness admits telling a lie, there is no need to leave
it just at that. The following example is from a murder trial. The
witness conceded that she had told a falsehood to her son, Russell,
to protect him.

> Were you trying to tell Russell the truth or not tell him the truth? —
>   Not tell him the truth.
> And you succeeded in that, didn't you? — I hope – hopefully.
> Now did you expect Russell to believe you? — Yes.
> Did you tell him in a way that you hoped would be believable? — Yes,
>   well I hope so, yes.
> Did you hope that you could convince him of the truth of what you
>   said? — Yes.
> And I suppose you thought that he wouldn't believe that his own mother
>   would tell him a lie, you were banking on that too, weren't you? —
>   Probably.
> He wouldn't believe his own mother would tell him a lie? — Probably
>   not.[3]

[6035] In *R v Anderson* the accused had confessed to rape. This
part of the cross-examination relied on two pieces of information.
The first was a DNA test for blood at the scene, which showed that
it could have come from the accused. The second was the note of
the sergeant of police who interviewed Mr Anderson. That note
showed that the sergeant told Mr Anderson that it was his blood.
The following cross-examination of the sergeant was on the *voir
dire*:

> You wanted to see him, did you, because of the results that you had got
>   from the forensic biologist? — That's correct.
> You were anxious, were you, to be accurate with him. That is, not to
>   mislead him in any way? — That's correct.
> To be quite fair with him? — Yes.
> And not to tell him a lie? — No.
> When he got back to the police station did you speak to him about the
>   blood? — Immediately, yes, I've started.
> Were you accurate with him? — Yes.

---

[3] *R v McConville*, (Supreme Court of Victoria). Cross-examination of Judith Anne Simmonds
    11 September 1989.

Did you say to him: "The results that we have show that the blood on the sheet could have come from you"? — I think I may have even said: "That was your blood." I may have been more specific.

If you'd said that, it was a lie, wasn't it, to your knowledge? — (no answer)

That was a lie, wasn't it? — Certainly it was not deliberately meant to be.

It was an accidental lie was it, not deliberate? — I believed what I said.

You believed it was his blood. Is that right? — I should phrase this correctly. It was an interrogatory lie.

I'm sorry? — I'm misleading the court. I didn't mean to intentionally do it. If it was an – if that is a lie, it was a lie . . .

It was an attitude, or a decision which you as an interrogator made because you thought you might that way derive from him an account of what took place? — Yes.

You didn't believe what you said was true? — That's correct.[4]

In this example the witness could have been directly confronted with the difference between the blood test and what he told the witness about it. The cross-examination derived more by inducing the witness to give a reason for the lie. It worked. The confession was excluded and the prosecution offered no evidence. Mr Anderson was acquitted.

[6040] In this final example, the witness was asked about a statement she had made to the police:

Did you give the information to the police in the hope that they would believe you? — Yes.

Did you deliver it in a way that you expected it to be believed? — Yes, I did.

And when you said (statement read) was that true or not true? — That was not true.[5]

Undermining a witness

[6045] The aim of most cross-examination of a witness who harms the case of an advocate is to undermine the evidence. The advocate may show that the evidence should not be accepted for any number of reasons. An identification may be suspect because the sighting was quick and it occurred at a time when the witness was frightened. An earwitness may not have heard things correctly.

---

[4] *R v Anderson* (1991) 1 NTLR 149; 57 A Crim R 143. See Chapter 5 [5065].

[5] *R v McConville* (above note 3). These three questions in cross-examination are non-leading.

[6050] The following example is taken from a libel action, *Cadbury v Daily News*, before a judge and jury in Birmingham, England, in 1909. The newspaper had accused Mr W. A. Cadbury of making profits from cocoa grown by slave labour on two islands off the coast of West Africa, one of which was San Thomé. In fact Mr Cadbury had hoped to improve the situation. Carson KC acted for the defendant. His cross-examination of Mr Cadbury is blistering and deadly. See how Carson watches the witness and adjusts his questions because of the answers:

Isn't it a fact that San Thomé cocoa has been slave grown to your knowledge for eight years? — Yes.

Was it slavery of a very atrocious character? — Yes.

The cocoa you were buying was procured by atrocious methods — Yes.

Men, women and children taken forcibly from their homes against their will? — Yes.

Were they marched on the road like cattle? — I cannot answer that question. They were marched in forced marches down the coast.

Were they labelled when they went on board ship? — Yes.

How far had they to march? — Various distances. Some came more than a thousand miles, some from quite near the coast.

Never to return again? — Never to return.

From the information that you procured, did they go down in shackles? — It is the usual custom, I believe, to shackle them at night.

Those who could not keep up with the march were murdered? — I have seen statements to that effect.

You do not doubt it? — I do not doubt that it has been so in some cases.

The men, women and children were freely bought and sold? — I do not believe . . . that there has been anything corresponding to the open slave markets of fifty years ago. It is more done by subtle trickery and arrangements of that kind.

You do not suggest that it is better because it is done by subtle trickery? — No.

The children born to the women who are taken out as slaves become the property of the owners of the slaves? — I believe that children born on the estates do.

Was it not the most cruel and atrocious form of slavery that ever existed? — I am not justified in distinguishing between slavery and slavery. All slavery is atrocious.

Knowing it was atrocious, you took the main portion of your supply of cocoa for the profit of your business from the islands conducted under this system? — Yes, for a period of some years.

You do not look on that as something immoral? — Not under the
circumstances.

[*Now the finish of a true artist.*]

Have you formed any estimate of the number of slaves who lost their
lives in preparing your cocoa during those eight years? — No, no, no.[6]

The jury found for the plaintiff and awarded damages of one far-
thing – then the smallest coin in the currency.[7]

Undermining one witness through another

[6055] The advocate who plans well will often try to damage the
evidence of one witness through that of another. How that damage
will be carried out depends on the way you plan it. Let us say that
there are two eyewitnesses to an event and that they live in the one
family. Simply asking "Did you and your sister talk about what you
both saw?" can be improved, perhaps by adding the following:

> Was her memory the same as yours?
> On every point?
> Did she notice anything that you had not noticed?
> Had you noticed anything that she had not?
> Did you agree on every single detail?[8]

Whatever the answers, there is fertile ground for comment. If the
siblings agree on every detail, they have probably got their heads
together, for two people rarely see the same things. If their evidence
disagrees, the earlier evidence that they had agreed on every point
cannot be true, and it is now impossible to say whether either of
them is correct.

[6060] The following example is from the 1947 murder trial of Frederick William McDermott. The case was unsuccessfully appealed to
the High Court.[9] A later inquiry exonerated Mr McDermott. An
earwitness was being cross-examined by defence counsel Frederick
Vizzard. She said in examination-in-chief that that she heard Mr
McDermott's de facto wife Florrie Hampton accuse Mr McDermott

---

[6] The transcript is referred to in E Marjoribanks, *Life of Lord Carson*, Vol 1, 1932, MacMillan,
London, pp. 395–397, and in H Montgomery Hyde, *Carson*, 1953, William Heinemann,
London, pp. 249–254.

[7] The re-examination by Rufus Isaacs is set out in Chapter 9 [9030].

[8] George Colman QC, *Cross-Examination*, 1970, Juta & Co, Cape Town, pp. 10–11.

[9] *McDermott v The King* (1948) 76 CLR 501.

of the murder of Mr Lavers. She said that Mr McDermott agreed
with the accusation.

> Now Florrie had been drinking, hadn't she? — Yes.
> And she was drinking a lot, wasn't she? — Yes.
> You had a big flagon of wine? — Yes.
> Show me how high off the ground it was? — It was four gallons.
> And Florrie was mad drunk that evening, wasn't she? — Yes.
> She hit Fred on the head with a bottle, didn't she? — Yes.
> What is she like when she is drunk, she is very abusive, isn't she? —
> Yes.
> And she is very nasty too, isn't she? — Yes.
> When she gets drunk she would say anything, wouldn't she? — Yes.
> She would accuse people of things too, wouldn't she? — Yes.
> And she has accused you of things that you didn't do? — Yes.
> Did you have any drink that night? — Yes, I did.[10]

Mr Vizzard must have taken the view about the witness that he
had to ask all leading questions. Sometimes you have to make that
decision based on your assessment of how best to handle the witness.
In the end, the prosecution did not call Florrie Hampton to give
evidence. Not surprising really, after this cross-examination, for it
must have had the aim of undermining Florrie's evidence. He used
one witness to undermine another.

[6065] Here is another example. Quentin Tipungwuti was charged
with murder. He made a full confession to the police, giving details of
the stab wounds to the deceased. He was a Tiwi man from Melville
Island. The prosecution called a police tracker to give evidence
of some of the relationships in that small community. On cross-
examination the witness said that he had been told by police where
the stab wounds were on the deceased's body, and that he had passed
that information on to the community. He said that the police had
asked him to bring the accused to the police station. He said in cross-
examination that the Tiwi name for policeman was *yiminipirne* –
man who gives you a flogging. The cross-examination continued:

> But in any event, when you picked Quentin up on the Monday, did you
> say to him in Tiwi words to this effect: "Look, the police want to see
> you; I'm picking you up because the detectives want to see you"? —
> Yes.

[10] Judge Eric Clegg, *Return Your Verdict* (Angus and Robertson, Sydney, 1965). In Chapter
5 "The Lavers Mystery", this cross-examination is on pages 72–73.

This is all in Tiwi you said that? — Yes

Did he say to you "Well, look, I don't really know what it's about because
    if the man was murdered I certainly didn't have anything to do with
    his death?" — Yes.

. . .

He asked you what it was all about and you said: "They told me to come
    and pick you up and take you back"? — Yes.

Did one of the police say to you: "Go down and pick up Quentin and
    bring him back here because I want to ask him some questions?" —
    Yes.[11]

When the police who questioned Quentin came to give evidence, the
jury seemed to be sceptical about the admissions he was said to have
made. The admissions were not made by a person with specialised
knowledge of the killing, for the information about the nature of
the wounds was freely available throughout the small community.

[6070] The facts leading up to the making of a statement to the
police can sometimes be used to weaken the evidence of the maker
of the statement and to undercut the prospective evidence of the
police. Here is an example:

Did they tell you that you could make a statement at the house? — No.

Did they tell you that you had to go with them? — Yes.

Did they tell you if you didn't go with them you might be arrested? —
    Yes.

And taken into custody? — Yes, they said they would charge me.

They would charge you? — Yes.

And was it your belief that you would be put into gaol with or without
    the chance of getting bail? — I didn't know what to think.

Yes? — I was just very frightened.[12]

In a criminal case it sometimes happens that a witness makes a
number of statements to the police. The later statements are asserted
to be true, if only because they fit the prosecution thesis of what
happened. The earlier statements, which are different, are claimed
to be false.

---

[11] *R v Quentin Tipungwuti* (Northern Territory Supreme Court, Darwin). Cross-
examination of Regis Pangaraminni 1 August 1989. Mr Tipungwuti was wholly acquitted.

[12] *R v McConville*, (Supreme Court of Victoria). Cross-examination of Judith Anne Simmonds, 11 September 1989.

Earlier failure to identify

[6075] Sometimes the advocate by careful preparation is able to discover that an identifying witness has had an earlier chance to identify the accused, and has failed. The preparation often means wading through a mass of material. A good example of a cross-examination that extracts the damaging consequences of the earlier failure to identify comes from *R v Fish and Swan*. The accused were police, charged with using violence on some young men and later telling lies about it on oath. Here is the cross-examination of one of the young men:

> You had never seen Swan before had you? — Before this night? No.
> Did you see him on the street? — No.
> So as far as in the garage was concerned there were a large number of men there? — That's correct.
> It was a traumatic occasion you say, you were being beaten? — That's correct.
> You were scared, frightened, is that correct? — Yes.
> And may we take it you were not looking around and saying: "I will remember that man again by his eyes, by his nose, by his mouth", I take it you were not doing that? — That's correct.
> So you say there was a man with a tie? — That's correct.
> But you would not recognise his face? — Sir, that man with the tie came into the office while I was sitting down and I had a better chance to look at his face then also to remember.
> So that is how you can say it is John Swan? — Yes.
> Why weren't you able to do that in 1995 at the Royal Commission? — I don't know, sir.
> No explanation for that? — No, I can't give you a reason why.[13]

Circumstantial evidence

[6080] A circumstantial case is often more potent than a case that relies on direct evidence. The reason is that direct evidence can often be met by denial or by rebutting it in other ways. A circumstantial case can have some of its evidential aspects refuted, yet still retain its force. Cross-examining in a circumstantial case is one that takes meticulous planning. For a defendant or an accused, the advocate's purpose is usually to raise an innocent hypothesis. For the plaintiff

---

[13] *R v Fish and Swan* (2002) 131 A Crim R 172 at 184–185 [57] (NSW CCA). The re-examination is at Chapter 9 [9050].

or prosecutor, the purpose is to reinforce the single conclusion on which the case rests.

[6085] In this example, Eugene Gorman KC was acting for Mrs Fitzpatrick, a widow. Her husband had been killed by a bag, which had slipped from the defendant's skip. Gorman tried to show *res ipsa loquitur* by strengthening the defendant's evidence. He lost, but not because of poor cross-examination.

> If a skip be properly tied nothing can fall from it. Is that right? — Yes, that is right.
>
> And are you certain of that? — Yes.
>
> I suppose you will agree that this man, Fitzpatrick, is dead? You know that, do you not? — Yes.
>
> And do you know that he was hit by a bag which fell from your skip. Do you agree with that? — Yes.
>
> . . .
>
> Tell us why the bag fell from the skip, seeing that you can make a skip fool-proof by proper tying? — I could not tell you. I do not know.
>
> You were on the skip? — Yes.
>
> You saw the bag fall? — I do now know how it happened, though.
>
> Does it occur to you that some of those knots may not have been tied with precision? — No, the knots were right.
>
> The wires were right? — Yes.
>
> The bags were right? — Yes.
>
> Everything was right, except Fitzpatrick. Everything was right was it not? Is that so? — Yes.
>
> Do you remember telling the Coroner that a load would not tilt because a dogman changed his position? — Yes.
>
> Your load did tilt, did it not? — Yes, it tilted.
>
> Had you previously known a properly tied load to tilt? — No.
>
> You will agree that it should not do it? — It should not do it, no.
>
> And the only reason why a load can tilt is if all those precautions were not taken, is it not? If there was something missing? — There was nothing missing.
>
> That is the only way in which a load can tilt, if there is something missing in the original tying? — Yes, I suppose so.[14]

[6090] In the trial of Hawley Harvey Crippen, the evidence was circumstantial.[15] Dr Crippen was an American living in England.

---

[14] *Fitzpatrick v Walter E Cooper Pty Ltd* (1935) 54 CLR 200 at 227–228.

[15] *R v Crippen* Oct 18–22, 1910, see Filson Young, *Trial of Hawley Harvey Crippen*, 1920, p. 112.

His wife had died and her body was mutilated, but the cause of death was probably poison. Dr Crippen had left England with his secretary named Ethel Le Neve.[16] They had become lovers. Dr Crippen was charged with his wife's murder. I have pointed earlier to the detailed preparation of the case for the prosecution by Richard Muir as being an example to us all.[17] So was his cross-examination of Dr Crippen. This extract is an excellent example of the short question, each containing one issue, and which erodes any alternative hypothesis:

> You thought you were in danger of arrest? — Yes.
> And so you fled the country? — Yes.
> Under a false name? — Yes.
> Shaved off your moustache? — Yes.
> Left off wearing your glasses in public? — Yes.
> Took Le Neve with you? — Yes.
> Under a false name? — Yes.
> Posing as your son? — Yes.
> Went to Antwerp? — Yes.

Dr Crippen told various people that his wife had gone to another man in America and later died. Muir cuts that defence to pieces:

> On the early morning of 1 February were you alone in your house with your wife? — Yes.
> Was she alive? — She was.
> And well? — She was.
> Do you know any person who has seen her alive since? — I do not.
> And do you know any person in the world who has had a letter from her since? — I do not.
> Do you know of any person who can prove any facts showing that she left your house alive? — Absolutely not.[18]

Previous convictions

[6095] Earlier convictions for dishonesty do not of themselves prove that the witness should not be believed. What is important is for

---

[16] Miss Le Neve was tried later and acquitted. The jury was out for only 20 minutes. She was represented by FE Smith KC who was afterwards Lord Birkenhead. Richard Muir again prosecuted.

[17] See Chapter 2 [2150].

[18] *R v Crippen*, Oct 18–22, 1910. See J H Phillips "Practical Advocacy" (1988) 62 ALJ 629 and (2003) 77 ALJ 725.

the fact-finder to be able to infer that the witness will have no qualms about telling a lie if it is to the witness's advantage. The prior convictions should be relevant to the case. Where a plaintiff says that the injuries were caused by the bad driving of the defendant, the defendant can be cross-examined about any other various traffic offences.[19] Those offences would not be relevant where the witness is said to be untruthful.

[6100] A trial in 2002 involved a prosperous man who ran a private hospital.[20] He had to dismiss two nurses for their dishonesty. Some time after their dismissal, they alleged that he came to the back of their house and damaged their car. He was charged with criminal damage. The defence was that they probably damaged the car themselves to implicate him and collect the insurance. The cross-examination of the first woman was centred on her dishonesty. It is not very often that you have this wealth of material. Note the number of non-leading questions:

Did you go to the (named) court on three charges of obtaining a Social Security benefit that was not payable? — Yes, I did.
At that time were you in employment? — Yes, I was.
Were you sentenced to four months' gaol and released on entering a $500 good behaviour bond for three years? — Yes, I was.
And ordered to pay $581 costs? — Yes, I was.
And to pay $4282 reparation? — Yes, I was.
Is that how much you'd stolen? — Yes.
How did you plead in that court? Did you plead guilty or not guilty? — Guilty.
You must have needed the money, did you, to cheat the Social Security? — I don't recall.
You don't know why you did it? — No, I don't recall.
[*Yes, there is more.*]
Been to gaol? — Yes, I have.
You were given two and a half years in gaol, weren't you? — That's correct.
The prosecution case was that you stole a blank bank cheque from a (named) bank where you were employed as a cleaner? — Correct.
They say you filled it out? — Correct.
For something in the order of $36,000? — Correct.
You took this cheque to (city named)? — Correct.

---

[19] *Bugg v Day* (1949) 79 CLR 442.
[20] The jury acquitted the man after a brief retirement.

Put it in the bank? — Correct.
And tried to withdraw the money? — Correct.
You told them, did you, that it was your winnings from Tatts? — Correct.
Was that the truth? — No.
You pleaded guilty? — Yes.
[*Yes, there is even more!*]
You tried to get money from a false insurance claim? — Correct.
Some electrical goods? — Yes.
Did you say that it was stolen? — Yes, I did.
Was that true? — No, it wasn't.
You reported it to the police too, didn't you? — Yes.
That it had been stolen? — Yes.
The report you made to the police? Yes? — That was false.
And you got convicted of it, didn't you — Yes, I did.
. . .
Have you been convicted under the name of Glenda Cook? — Yes, I have.
Was Glenda Cook your real name? — No, it was not.

Bad reputation

[6105] A witness can give evidence that another witness has a reputation for dishonesty and that the witness would not believe the other's word oath. In jurisdictions where such evidence is allowed, the questions, even in cross-examination, must only be as follows:

Do you know Mr William Black?
Do you know people who know him?
What is his reputation for telling the truth?
Would you believe him on his oath?[21]

In a criminal case I was defending, I asked one prosecution witness about the reputation for truth of the principal prosecution witness. When I asked the last question, "Would you believe him on his oath?" his reply was, "If he swore to me that it was raining, I would want to go outside and check for myself."

[6110] This evidence is rarely used, partly because few advocates know that it is admissible.

---

[21] *R v Hanrahan* (1964) 87 WN (NSW) 458 [1967] 2 NSWLR 717; *R v Richardson* [1969] 1 QB 299; *Bell v The Queen* (1985) 7 FCR 555 at 563.

[6115] A person's reputation for violence is admissible where an accused claims to have acted in self-defence against that person, or acted under duress because of fear of the person.[22] Cross-examination of any witness on the subject is in the ordinary way, with such leading questions as are necessary.

Child witnesses

[6120] Cross-examination of a child calls for great delicacy. You must be gentle in manner and fairly softly spoken. Try to ask as few leading questions as possible.[23]

The witness who always agrees

[6125] Occasionally, a witness agrees with everything the cross-examiner asks. After the trial the advocate will take congratulations for the answers the witness has given. But in these rare cases the cross-examiner can do no wrong. The following is a cross-examination in a rape case:

> What Ms Moore says is that you said to her that [N] forced himself on you. That was not true, was it? — No.
> Because he didn't threaten you, did he? — No, he didn't.
> Certainly was not physical towards you, was he? — No.
> What I suggest what you were concerned about or unhappy about, you were unhappy that he had come inside of you, weren't you? — Like I was not happy about that?
> Yes? — Yes.
> You knew he was going to have sex with you? — Yes, I did.
> That was not a problem, was it? You were happy for that to happen? — Yes.
> But because he came in you that made you angry, didn't it? — Yes.
> That is the reason you complained, wasn't it? — Yes.[24]

Invention and recent invention

[6130] Beware of asking a witness if the evidence has just been made up. The risk is this: if the witness has made an earlier statement, spoken or written, your opponent in re-examination can introduce

---

[22] *R v Gibb and McKenzie* [1983] 2 VR 155.
[23] See Chapter 2 [2200].
[24] *R v NJM* (2001) 126 A Crim R 378 at 383 (Vic CA).

that earlier statement in rebuttal. If you do want to allege that the witness has invented the whole of the evidence from start to finish, ask it in that form safely. It may be one of the few times when your question will contain more than one issue.

[6135] Follow the example of Marie Shaw QC.[25] She alleged a total invention and because of that, her formulation was held on appeal not to have suggested recent invention. The question she asked was this:

> I suggest you made up these conversations that you say you had with Shane at "The Venue". You made up those statements that he confessed to the murder of his own father for your own vindictive purposes and just to save your own skin. You dispute that? — I dispute that.[26]

[6140] The effects of an allegation of recent invention in cross-examination will be dealt with under re-examination.[27]

Summary

[6145] Here is a summary of the propositions on cross-examination:

1. Use simple English.
2. Keep questions short. Include one issue only in each question.
3. Be polite. Don't argue with the witness, the bench or your opponent.
4. Keep control over the witness. Leading questions are permitted but use non-leading questions where possible such as where you are sure of the answer, or where the answer does not matter.
5. Watch the witness and listen to the answers. Tailor the rest of your cross-examination accordingly.
6. Where an inference your way is clearly open, don't ask the witness to agree with it. The witness may disagree, giving good reasons. The question is unnecessary and is one question too many.

---

[25] Later Judge Shaw, South Australian District Court.
[26] *R v Martin (No 2)* (1997) 68 SASR 419; 94 A Crim R 357. (I suggest you omit the words "I suggest". See above Chapter 5 [5080] and following).
[27] See Chapter 9 [9065] – [9075].

7. Comply with the rule in *Browne v Dunn*. Never say "I put it to you", "I suggest to you" or "My client will say". Ask questions that call for answers of fact.
8. Learn by heart the rules of cross-examination on documents. Until then you can safely use a document as if it were inadmissible by asking five questions:
   • Look at this document (handing it to the witness).
   • Don't tell us what it is.
   • Read it to yourself.
   • Hand it back.
   • Do you still stick to your evidence?
9. If it suits your purpose:
   • Draw out every damaging detail.
   • Turn one lie into a tissue of lies.
   • Cut off the chance of escape, then put contradictions one by one.
   • Set one witness against another.
10. Finish on a good answer or a series of them.

Chapter 7

Cross-examination of experts

Opinion evidence

[7000] Witnesses can only give evidence of what has been derived from the senses: what they saw, or heard, or smelt, or touched or tasted. But experts are in a class of their own. An expert can give evidence of opinion. That opinion must be in a field of specialised knowledge, and the witness must have gained expertise in that field through training, study or experience. The facts on which an expert bases an opinion must be identified.[1]

[7005] Before you cross-examine an expert you will need to do a great deal of preparation. With a lay witness you can use your knowledge of human affairs and your courtroom experience. With an expert it is quite different. The advocate starts from an inferior position. Without careful preparation the advocate will not be able to detect fallacies, oversights, exaggerations, evasions or distortions. With diligence you will be able to master sufficient expertise. To put it another way, if the advocate with perseverance cannot follow the expert's propositions, neither will the court.

[7010] The sorts of matters you will have to look at are the following:

1. Read and make sure you understand the expert's report.
2. Get comfortable with the expert's terms and jargon and their proper pronunciation.
3. Read as much as you can on the subject.
4. If necessary get the advice of your own expert.
5. Try translating the expert's terms into ordinary words, easily understood.

---

[1] *Makita (Australia) Pty Ltd v Sprowles* (2001) 52 NSWLR 705 (CA) per Heydon JA at 743–744 [85].

6. Is the evidence admissible? Do you need to cross-examine?
7. Is the witness an expert giving an opinion in the expert's field of expertise?
8. Has the expert been given all the exhibits and examined everything relevant? Has the expert made the correct factual assumptions?
9. Has the expert looked at all the contemporary notes so as to form a proper opinion?
10. Has the expert taken into account anything extraneous or inadmissible?

Is the witness an expert?

[7015] The witness may not be an expert at all. If the jury can work everything out for itself the witness is no expert. So if a bank produces a photograph of armed robbers, the police are not experts in identification. They are no better than the jury at identifying one of the robbers as the accused.[2] No witness, not even an expert, can give inadmissible evidence. So in a sexual assault case a psychologist cannot give evidence that the complainant had been sexually assaulted, not by the accused, but by another person.[3] Nor can the psychologist explain why the evidence of a child may contain contradictions – what has been called "accommodation syndrome".[4] If an expert omits the basis for an opinion, the evidence is liable to be excluded.[5]

[7020] If you have a real doubt about whether your opponent's expert is an expert, or whether the evidence is admissible, you should ordinarily raise the matter with the judge before the hearing starts. What you seek is a ruling that your opponent cannot lead that evidence.

[7025] The alternative is to undermine the expertise of the witness. George Maxwell KC had to cross-examine a pathologist who had performed the autopsy on the victim. The conclusion of the expert was that death was due to poisoning from two doses of arsenic. Maxwell began this way:

---

[2] *Smith v The Queen* (2001) 206 CLR 650.
[3] *HG v The Queen* (1999) 197 CLR 414.
[4] *R v C* (1993) 60 SASR 467; *R v F* (1995) 83 A Crim R 502.
[5] *Makita (Australia) Pty Ltd v Sprowles* (2001) 52 NSWLR 705 (CA).

You have been a government pathologist for a good many years, have
you not? — I have been Pathologist to the Coroner. That is very much
the same thing.

And your practice, so to speak, has been for the most part among dead
bodies rather than live bodies? — That is so.

Have you had much experience in diagnosing living subjects within
the last 20 or 30 years? — Not from the bedside – only from the
laboratory.

Your attention has been more concentrated upon ascertaining post-
mortem conditions and then reasoning back from these as to what
the history of that case must have been? — Yes.[6]

Cross-examining

[7030] You must cross-examine properly, as you would with any
witness. Make sure you don't hand control to the witness by asking
non-leading questions on central issues. An example of giving the
witness such an opportunity occurred in a possession of cannabis
case. Was the substance cannabis? In cross-examination the defence
advocate asked:

So, it is something else that tells you it is cannabis resin? — That's
correct.

What is that? — It is appearance, the presence of fragments of plant
material which are consistent with what you would expect to find
where plants have been extracted in a crude way with regard to their
resinous substance.[7]

The appeal court used this evidence to show the proof of the substance and to dismiss the accused's appeal.

[7035] The cross-examination of a firearms expert by Phillip Opas
QC provides a good example of giving an expert no leeway. The
pre-trial preparation comes through.

It is fully automatic in the sense that it is self-loading? — That is so.
Gas operated? — Yes.
And it has no recoil? — Very little.

---

[6] *R v Griggs* (Supreme Court of Victoria, Sale, 7 March 1928): A J Buchanan, *Famous Australian Trials: The Trial of Ronald Geeves Griggs*, 1930, Law Book Co, Sydney, pp. 98–99.
The jury disagreed. At the retrial in Melbourne, Reverend Griggs was acquitted.

[7] *R v Symons* (1988) 32 A Crim R 370 at 374.

Well, no noticeable recoil? — That is so.
And you could fire it all day without getting a sore shoulder? — Yes.[8]

Proving mistakes

[7040] Experts make mistakes. If you have done the preparation you might be able to prove it. *R v Taktak*[9] is a good example. Gregory Scragg cross-examined a pathologist on the estimate of the time of death. It was a most important trial issue. Mr Taktak had arranged prostitutes for a drug dealer. Sometime later the dealer told the accused to collect one of the women who was ill. The accused did. The woman died from a drug overdose. Whether Mr Taktak was guilty of manslaughter by criminal negligence depended on how long he and the woman were together, which showed the importance of the time of death. Mr Scragg's enormous preparation is evident. First he induced the pathologist to take earliest time of death from 7.30 am back to between 4.30 am and 5.30 am. Then he got to work.

At the time you made your post mortem you were not aware of the variables that existed at the time of death and following death as to, say, environmental factors and the clothing of the body, is that right? — That is so.

No one came to you and told you what the temperature of the room was in which the body was found, is that right? — That is so.

No one told you whether the body had been clothed or unclothed after death, is that right? — I can't remember the actual conversation that took place at the time, I am afraid, so I can't be sure of that.

If the girl had been clothed after death, that would take the earliest point of time at which death may have occurred even further back, would you agree with that? — Not necessarily.

[*He tries another approach.*]

Well, if I could put it to you this way: if there were certain variables that indicated that the body was in such an environment as to keep it, say, warmer than might otherwise be the case? — Yes.

...

But if the air was warm, if the body was clothed, if one was to accept those two assumptions for the moment? — Yes.

---

[8] Opas QC defending in the trial *R v Ryan* in March 1966 before Starke J and jury: Patrick Tennison, *Defence Counsel*, 1975, Hill of Content, Melbourne, p. 129.

[9] *R v Taktak* (1988) 14 NSWLR 226; 34 A Crim R 334.

Could that not have the effect of making the earliest time at which death occurred earlier than the 4.30 to 5.30 am range? — Yes, taken on its own, yes.[10]

The cross-examination then turned to the subjects of rigor mortis and lividity. Not surprisingly, the Court of Criminal Appeal held that the evidence as to the likely time of death was unsatisfactory.[11] The appeal was allowed and a verdict of acquittal entered.

Using the simple example

[7045] Experts will often give evidence only of their opinion. It is often valuable to use a simple concrete illustration to test that opinion. In the following example an expert was giving evidence for the plaintiff in a case in which she said she slipped on stairs. The expert tested the stairs for the co-efficient of friction but it was nine years after the accident. The defendant's advocate cross-examined.

No doubt you have seen many occasions when people walking down-stairs miss their footing, no problems with the stairs, they just lose their footing? — Yes.
And that may have happened here if the co-efficient of friction was different to the time when you tested the shoe? — That is always possible, yes.[12]

Asking one expert about the opinion of another

[7050] If you are intending to contradict the opinion of an expert by later evidence, or in your submissions, you must give the expert an opportunity to answer the proposed contradiction. This rule of practice is known as the rule in *Browne v Dunn*. That rule has been examined earlier.[13]

[7055] In *R v Hughes* the accused was charged with murder. He shot the victim twice. The shots were about five minutes apart. There were excellent defences to the first shot. When the second shot was

---

[10] *R v Taktak* at 231; 338–339.
[11] *R v Taktak* at 229; 337.
[12] *Makita (Australia) Pty Ltd v Sprowles* (2001) 52 NSWLR 705 at 726. See also Chapter 4 [4070].
[13] See Chapter 5 [5075]–[5090].

fired, one possibility was that the victim was already dead from the first shot. The defence advocates had advice from the pathologist Dr R. B. Collins that you could not exclude the possibility that the victim was dead when the second shot was fired. Dr Collins later gave that evidence. The prosecution's pathologist gave evidence that the victim was alive when the second shot was fired. The defence cross-examination had to give him a chance to comment on the evidence that the defence intended to call. Here is part of the cross-examination:

> The doctors have a phrase to describe the time that surrounds the time of death? — Yes.
> They have a phrase that they call the peri-mortem period, do they not? — Yes.
> Where they say, "Well, we don't know when death occurs but that peri-mortem period is a couple of minutes either side of the death"? — Yes.
> And the doctors say about that, do they, that even though death occurs some time in that peri-mortem period, they can't say precisely when? — No.
> It is too fine a judgment for a doctor to make? — Yes.
> That's something for the Almighty? — I agree.[14]

[7060] Sometimes the expert will agree with the opinion put in cross-examination. That agreement may make it unnecessary to call your own expert. Dan O'Gorman[15] was defending in a murder case. He cross-examined a psychiatrist called by the prosecution. The witness had obviously read the reports of other psychiatrists and had those reports with him in the witness box.

> You're aware of Professor Peter Yellowlees? — Yes.
> He is a fellow psychiatrist? — Yes.
> He is the professor in the Department of Psychiatry at the University of Queensland? — Yes.
> He is of the highest standing, isn't he? — He is indeed.
> Yes . . . have you seen his report? — I have. I've read it, yes.
> Do you have a copy there? — I think I do. Yes.
> Could I ask you to go to page 6 please? — Page 6.

---

[14] *R v Hughes* (Supreme Court of Victoria) 17 July 1990.
[15] Later O'Gorman SC.

"I certainly agree that at the time of the killing Cooper was deprived of the capacity to understand what he was doing and I believe the primary cause of his deprivation was intoxication with alcohol and benzodiazepine." You would agree with it in view of what you now know, wouldn't you, doctor? — I think that's the most likely scenario, yes, from what I know.[16]

Turning the witness your way

[7065] With careful preparation, an expert witness called by your opponent can be turned your way. Some experts have fixed standpoints, but many regard themselves as true professionals. Take the case of Andre Chayna. She was charged with three murders. The victims were her two children and her sister-in-law. The only issue was her mental state. The prosecution called a psychiatrist. Stephen Norrish QC was the defence advocate.[17] As in all of these cases with expert evidence, the huge amount of preparation is obvious. There was evidence from seven psychiatrists. Three said that Mrs Chayna was insane and three said she had diminished responsibility. The seventh was Dr Skinner who said she was normal. Later Norrish QC was able to show that Dr Skinner's opinion was not soundly based for she had not taken into account the proper facts of the case.

[7070] In the following extract from his cross-examination Norrish QC got complete agreement from Dr Skinner:

To tell your child that you are going to read them a book and to close their eyes and then stab them in the throat and the chest, that is very disturbed thinking? — It is extremely disturbed.

Reflecting again either an abnormal mind at the time or a defect of reason on her part. That's correct isn't it? — Yes.

And if that abnormality or defect on her part was a consequence of a major depression, it would explain her conduct in killing the children? — Yes.

And even on your history from her of her reasons for killing the children, her reasons are totally inappropriate to the circumstances? — Oh, yes.

. . .

---

[16] *R v Cooper* (Supreme Court of Queensland). Cross-examination of Dr Flanagan 19 May 2003.

[17] Later Judge Norrish QC of New South Wales District Court.

But when she says that the only way out is to kill them and she plans that over a period of time it reflects, doesn't it, a very disturbed state of mind? — Yes, it reflects a severe abnormality of mind.[18]

[7075] Another example is using an expert's other papers in cross-examination. Siobhan Herbert did that in a case about recovered memory. On *voir dire* the defence called a psychiatrist to show the fallibility of the complainant's evidence of a sexual assault that occurred 25 years before. Ms Herbert, prosecuting, prepared her cross-examination by finding other articles written by the doctor. Not surprisingly, he agreed with the questions based on these articles. Note the sweet brevity of the questions.

And you would agree that some of the techniques that can result in recovered memories are the use of self-help books? — Correct.
Hypnosis? — Correct.
Guided imagery? — Correct.
Inner child work? — Correct.
Dream analysis? — Correct.
Body work? — Correct.[19]

Not testing important items

[7080] It sometimes happens that the expert has failed to do something important, such as carrying out a test on an item significant in the case. Where the expert has failed to perform the obvious, the cross-examination needs only to point to the omission. Here is the cross-examination of a police officer by Hastings KC, defending a murder case:

Immediately upon your arrival at the flat the prisoner told you, did he not, that there had been a struggle and that it was the dead man who fired the first shot? — Yes.
If his story was true, from the position in which the two men must have been standing, you would have expected to find the mark of a bullet on the window? — Yes.
Was there such a bullet mark on the window? — Yes.

---

[18] *R v Chayna* (1993) 66 A Crim R 178 at 184–185. She was convicted. Norrish QC ran the appeal. The Court of Appeal set aside the murder convictions and entered manslaughter convictions because of diminished responsibility.

[19] Referred to by the New South Wales Court of Criminal Appeal in *R v Glossop* [2001] NSWCCA 165 (4 May 2001) at [40]. (In the end the prosecution case failed due in no small measure to the efforts of defence counsel Charles Waterstreet.)

If the prisoner's story is true, the dead man must at some time have held the revolver in his hand? — Yes.

In that case you would have expected to find the dead man's fingerprints upon the revolver? — Possibly.

And if those fingerprints were on the revolver, that would be a vital piece of evidence for the defence? — (no answer recorded).

Were the dead man's fingerprints on that revolver? — I don't know.

Why not? Is it not the duty of the police to search for fingerprints? Were they ever taken in this case? — No.

Why not? Why not? Has somebody made a grave mistake? — (no answer).[20]

[7085] Often it is no fault of the expert for not examining something important. In a criminal case the police decide which evidence will be sent for testing and which not. Here is an example of police not asking the expert to examine some of the items. Quentin Tipungwuti was charged with murder. He made his denials sufficiently clear. He had no motive. Others did. One of those with a motive and opportunity was a man called Tractor Joe. The police had seized his knife and his shorts and had a swab taken of his blood. The defence arranged their tender as exhibits. None of these items was sent for analysis. Tractor Joe's shorts had a large stain on them. The defence had set the scene that Tractor Joe was more likely than the accused to be the killer. Here is the cross-examination of the biologist:

Ms Kuhl, I wonder if you can have a look at the knife in the sheath which is exhibit P8, I think. You've never been asked to examine that, have you? — No, I haven't.

Likewise, in this investigation, did all the materials you get come from a man called Senior Constable Neiman? — That's correct, yes.

. . .

I've just been handed a pair of shorts. You didn't examine these shorts, did you? — No, the shorts that I've just looked at had my number on it; they were the ones I examined.

[*Counsel holds up the heavily stained shorts.*]

You're not able to tell with the naked eye whether there are blood stains on these, are you? — I test stains that might be blood. I won't ever say they are blood just by the naked eye.

---

[20] Patrick Hastings, *Cases in Court*, 1949, William Heinemann, London, pp. 288–290. The story loses nothing in the telling.

Just have a look at the stain on the back. Does that look like it might
  be blood? — It's possible. It could be grease, it could be dirt, but I
  wouldn't know until I tested it.
No, but you can't dismiss the possibility of blood? — No.
[*Shorts identified as belonging to Tractor Joe are tendered.*]
Can I take it also, Ms Kuhl, from what you've told us that you were never
  shown a swab? Mr Neiman never handed you a swab for analysis? —
  No, the only things he handed me were those listed in my report.
The things that you've told us about? — Yes.[21]

Not looking at contemporary notes

[7090] An expert should look at contemporary notes. Sometimes a
witness does not look at the witness's own notes taken at the time.
The good advocate will discover whether the result is a taxing of
memory that leads to mistakes. Generally the witness has not looked
at the contemporary notes of others. An expert will often reserve a
final opinion in order to digest those notes. The cross-examination
will emphasise what the expert has not been shown.[22]

The expert with bias

[7095] Occasionally an expert witness is biased. An example of the
cross-examination of such a witness comes from T. W. Smith QC.[23]
As a young Victorian barrister he defended an industrial company
before a magistrate on the charge of using what was called a "crank
press" without the prescribed guard. This was Smith's account of
the case:

> The defence was that the machine in question was not a "crank
> press". When the inspector got into the box, he produced a picture
> of the machine in question and said it was a "crank press". When I
> came to cross-examine him I showed him two or three other pictures
> of what, according to my instructions, were genuine crank presses;
> he hardly glanced at them, but denounced them as not being crank
> presses. Then I had an idea and passed him his own exhibit. He
> treated it in exactly the same way; he gave it the same quick look and
> said, "No, that's not one either". So I was able to pass the document
> to the magistrate and asked him to look at the back of it and sat

---

[21] *R v Tipungwuti* (Northern Territory Supreme Court, Darwin) 9 August 1989.

[22] See, for example *Shorey v PT Ltd* (2003) 77 ALJR 1104 at [81] and [82].

[23] TW Smith QC became Smith J of the Victorian Supreme Court 1950–1973.

down. The prosecution was never able to extricate itself from that situation.[24]

This cross-examination was ingenious. The decision to show the witness his own picture was made, as Clarence Darrow said, "in the twinkling of an eye".[25]

[24] (1983) 57 Law Institute of Victoria Journal 813.
[25] See Chapter 1 [1045].

Chapter 8

Cross-examination on documents

Best and worst aspects

[8000] This is the fourth chapter on cross-examination. As we have already seen, it is quite possible that when you cross-examine any one witness you may need to draw on a range of skills and techniques. Sometimes you must use documents.

[8005] There are usually three main purposes in cross-examining on documents:

1. Proving a document that you want to tender.
2. Proving a fact in a document, without necessarily tendering it.
3. Using a document to discredit a witness.

[8010] The rules of cross-examination on documents are complex and technical.[1] It can be a minefield. At worst, an inadmissible prejudicial document can be tendered as real evidence against your client. At best, the cross-examination of a witness on a document can turn a difficult case totally your way.

[8015] The purpose of this chapter is to examine some of the tricky aspects of cross-examination on documents. The first part contains many of the main rules. The second part covers how to avoid some of the main traps. The third part is how to cross-examine on a document to your advantage. The second and third aspects are in addition to the techniques set out in the previous chapters.

---

[1] See McHugh QC "Cross-Examination on Documents" (1985) 1 Aust Bar Rev 51–68; David Ross QC "Techniques and duties in cross-examination" (2005) 27 Aust Bar Rev 84–104.

Some rules

[8020] *Queen's Case*[2] still has some application. Queen Caroline was accused of adultery. The Lords held that during the cross-examination of a witness about an earlier statement in writing, the document must be shown to the witness *and* put into evidence by the cross-examiner. The second part of the rule was regarded as too harsh. It meant that previous consistent statements were put into evidence. Further, defence counsel lost the right of final address. In those days the civil rules applied in a criminal case: that is, if the defence adduced evidence the prosecutor had the right of last address.[3] The decision ruined cross-examination on documents. Legislation was passed in England to ameliorate the position.[4] Equivalent legislation was passed in Australia[5] and elsewhere.[6] That legislation now provides that the cross-examiner brings the circumstances of the inconsistent statement to the notice of the witness. The effect of the legislation is that the document does not have to be shown to the witness. Nor does it have to be tendered.

[8025] Nevertheless you must have the document in court or capable of being produced. *R v Anderson*[7] is a cautionary tale. It was a fraud case. The accused gave evidence. The prosecutor in cross-examination held up a document and asked if the accused had made the document admitting indebtedness. It was denied. The appeal succeeded. There was no such document. By the proviso to the *Evidence Acts* and from the cases it is clear that the trial judge retains a discretion to require the production of the document and its tender.[8] It is likely that even if you cross-examine on an identified

---

[2] *Queen's Case* (1820) 2 Brod & B 284; 22 RR 662; 129 ER 696 (HL).

[3] In a criminal case it may be different in the Code jurisdictions when evidence is called on facts. See David Ross QC, *Ross on Crime*, 3rd ed., 2007, Lawbook Co, Sydney, at [1.2230]. Likewise Canada: *Criminal Code* s.651. In New Zealand in a criminal case the defence always addresses last: *Crimes Act 1961* (NZ) s.367.

[4] *Criminal Procedure Act 1865* s.5.

[5] The present legislation is *Uniform Evidence Acts* (Cth, NSW & Tas) s.43; *Evidence Act 1958* (Vic) s.36; *Evidence Act 1977* (Qld) s.19; *Evidence Act 1929* (SA) s.29; *Evidence Act 1906* (WA) s.22; *Evidence Act* (NT) s.20; *Evidence Act 1971* (ACT) s.62.

[6] *Indian Evidence Act 1872* s. 145; *Evidence Act 1872* (Bangladesh) s. 145; *Evidence Act 1950* (Malaysia) s. 145; *Evidence Act 1908* (New Zealand) s. 11; *Evidence Act 1985* (Canada) s. 10.

[7] *R v Anderson* (1929) 21 Cr App R 178.

[8] The *Evidence Acts* and *Alchin v Commissioner for Railways* (1935) 35 SR (NSW FC) 498 at 509 per Jordan CJ; *Wood v Desmond* (1958) 78 WN 65 (FC) at 67; *Hrysikos v Mansfield* (2002) 5 VR 485; 135 A Crim R 179 (CA) at 505 per Eames JA; 199 [75].

document and ask whether the witness still sticks to the evidence you may have to undertake to put the document in evidence.[9]

[8030] If the witness denies or does not distinctly admit the earlier statement it can be proved. The proof may be confined to the words the cross-examiner wants to use.

Calling for a document

[8035] Call for your opponent's document at your peril, for if you use the wrong procedure you may be forced to tender the document. Simply calling for a document in your opponent's possession and reading it entitles your opponent to tender it as an exhibit, with all the ramifications that has. There is a way around it. You can use a document to refresh the memory of a witness. In a criminal case it may be a statement or a committal deposition or a diary entry. Nothing unusual about that. If, however, you call for a document from the other side, which the witness had used to refresh memory and you cross-examine on parts not used to refresh the memory of the witness, you may be required to tender the document. This happens very rarely in a criminal case because of the prosecution's duty to serve relevant documents on the defence. In a criminal case it will happen the following way, if at all. If the prosecution should have given the document to the defence, the prosecutor cannot call for its tender.[10]

[8040] You suspect that the other side has some sort of private document, which has not been identified and may not have to be. You want to see it because you think you may be able to use it to your advantage. You are conscious of the rule that if you call for a document in the hands of the other side and inspect it, you may be required to tender it as an exhibit.[11] To avoid that risk you do

---

[9] McHugh QC doubted this proposition. It comes from *R v Jack* (1894) 15 LR (NSW) 196. The proposition finds some support in *Alchin v Commissioner for Railways* (1935) 35 SR (NSW FC) 498 at 509, which in turn was supported in *R v Fraser* (1995) 65 SASR 260; 85 A Crim R 385 (CCA) at 266–267; 390–391 per Doyle CJ and *J Boag & Son Brewing Ltd v Bridon Investments Pty Ltd* (2001) 10 Tas R 26 at 33 [13] (Slicer J). But *R v Jack* was criticised in *Madison v Goldrick* (1976) 1 NSWLR 651 at 660.

[10] *R v Weatherstone* (1968) 12 FLR 14 (ACT, Smithers J); *R v Moore* (1995) 77 A Crim R 577 at 582–583 (NSW CCA).

[11] *Walker v Walker* (1937) 57 CLR 630 at 636 per Dixon J; *Senat v Senat* [1965] P 172 at 177; *R v Harrison* [1966] VR 72 at 76 (CCA); *R v McGregor* [1984] 1 Qd R 256; 11 A Crim R 148 (CCA); *J Boag & Son Brewing Ltd v Bridon Investments Pty Ltd* (2001) 10 Tas R 26 at 31 [10] (Slicer J).

the following things. First, you identify the document. Second, you establish that the witness used it to refresh memory. Third, you call for it without running the risk of having to tender it. Fourth, you read it. Fifth, you cross-examine on it. My only suggestions on technique are these. Non-leading questions are often the better way. And the term "refresh your memory" may not be as effective for many witnesses. Instead use "bring things back to mind" or "help you remember" or "remind you".

> Did you make a (statement)?
> (What was it?)
> When did you make it?
> Was that very soon after?
> Did you look at it again?
> Did you look at it before giving evidence today?
> Did it bring things back to mind? OR Did it help you remember?
>   OR did it remind you of what happened?
> I call for that (document).

You call for the statement with impunity and cross-examine on it. The safest course is to examine the document first, that is, before the case starts. You can get most documents by subpoena, or notice to produce.

[8045] There is another risk. Do not ask the witness to refresh memory from the statement, then assail the witness for what is not included in the statement. That will entitle your opponent to call for its tender[12] during your cross-examination, or even later.[13]

Cross-examining on inadmissible documents

[8050] Sometimes you may want to cross-examine on a document that is not admissible. For example, it may not be the document of the witness. It may be the statement of another witness,[14] or a police report.[15] It may be an extract from a newspaper.[16] Where the

---

[12] *Hrysikos v Mansfield* (2002) 5 VR 485 at 504–505 [73]–[75].

[13] *R v McGregor* [1984] 1 Qd R 256; 11 A Crim R 148 at 265; 152–153 (CCA); *R v Foggo; Ex parte Attorney General (Qld)* [1989] 2 Qd R 49; *J Boag & Son Brewing Ltd v Bridon Investments Pty Ltd* (2001) 10 Tas R 26 at 33 [15] (Slicer J); *Alexander v Manley* (2004) 29 WAR 194.

[14] *R v Trotter* (1982) 7 A Crim R 8 at 19.

[15] *R v Seham Yousry* (1914) 11 Cr App R 13 at 18.

[16] *R v Bedington* [1970] Qd R 353.

document is not admissible you must not identify it or suggest its nature or contents.[17] You simply ask five questions:

> Look at this document.
> Don't tell us what it is.
> Read it to yourself.
> Now hand the document back please.
> Do you still stick to what you said?[18]

[8055] If the witness is likely to have seen the document before (for example, a newspaper report) the cross-examiner can ask:

> Have you seen that document before?
> Were you aware of (the circumstances referred to in the article) at the relevant time?
> (If yes) Do you accept the facts stated?[19]

Using a document to discredit a witness

[8060] The defence may have two purposes in using a document to discredit a witness. The first is obvious: to set the scene for a later address to the jury that the witness is an admitted liar. The second is more subtle. It may enable cross-examination of a later witness, such as a police officer. The cross-examination of the later police witness will be designed to show partiality by deciding which statement is true and which is not, and to show that the statement the officer selected as true was the one that best fitted the prosecution thesis. In this example from a murder trial, the witness had made a number of different statements:

> The formal parts of this statement again said "I hereby acknowledge that this statement is true and correct. I make it in the belief that a person making a false statement in the circumstances is liable to the penalties of perjury"? — Yes.
> And you again signed that did you? — Yes.

---

[17] *R v Bedington* [1970] Qd R 353 at 359–360; *R v Alexander and McKenzie* (2002) 6 VR 53 at 75–76 [45]–[46].

[18] In *R v Orton* [1922] VLR 469 at 470, Cussen J said, "The witness should have been . . . asked to the effect 'Having looked at the document do you still adhere to your former statement.'" See also *R v Trotter* (1982) 7 A Crim R 8 at 22. See also *Uniform Evidence Acts* s.44.

[19] Malcolm QC, "Cross-examination on Documents" (1986) 2 Aust Bar Rev 267 at 273.

You again signed that notation that you were prepared to render yourself liable to the penalties of perjury? — Yes.

Have you been charged with perjury? — No.

Have the police told you that you are going to be charged with perjury? — No.

Have you been charged with making a false statement to the police? — No.

Have you been told that you are going to be charged with making a false statement to the police? — No.[20]

Prior inconsistent statement

[8065] A witness will sometimes give evidence-in-chief that is inconsistent with what the witness had said before. This earlier account is called a prior (or previous) inconsistent statement. The inconsistency must be about an issue in the case, but that can include whether the witness is giving an honest and accurate account. The previous statement can be written or spoken.

[8070] There are some rules of practice about cross-examining on that prior inconsistent statement. The first is that what was said earlier must be brought to the attention of the witness. The second rule is that if the witness admits the prior statement, it cannot be proved and the cross-examination proceeds.[21] If the witness does not admit the prior statement, then it can be proved. If necessary the witness is stood down and the proving witness interposed.[22] A prior inconsistent statement affects the credibility of the witness. Is the evidence believable? These propositions apply in civil and in criminal cases. In criminal cases, the proof of a prior inconsistent statement is usually fairly easy. If the witness signed a statement to the police, that can easily be proved. If the witness said something different at the committal, the prosecution will invariably admit the correctness of the depositions.

[8075] A good way to get the maximum effect from a prior incon-sistent statement is to give the witness no means of escape and then

---

[20] *R v McConville* (Supreme Court of Victoria) 11 September 1989.

[21] *R v Soma* (2003) 212 CLR 299 per McHugh J at 316–317 [55]–[56].

[22] *Cheney v The Queen* (1991) 28 FCR 103; 99 ALR 360 (FCA) per von Doussa J at 122–126; 379–383.

ask the ultimate questions. Here is an example from a criminal case in 2002:[23]

> While he was at the back did you watch him for very long? — Yes, I did.
>
> Did he seem to know what he was doing? — He seemed dazed.
>
> You're quite sure you saw him? — I certainly did.
>
> You're quite sure it wasn't somebody else? — No, it wasn't.
>
> You wouldn't have said earlier, would you, that you didn't see him at all that night? — No.
>
> Do you remember the questions you were asked at committal? — Possibly not all. You'd have to jog my memory.
>
> Did you say there at all that you didn't see (naming accused) that night? — No, I didn't.
>
> You gave evidence at the committal, didn't you? — Yes, I did.
>
> On April 24 last year? — Yes.
>
> Were you asked this question and did you give this answer, "...whatever you say you saw on that night, you never saw (naming accused) did you?" Answer "No." Was that question asked and that answer given? — I don't remember.
>
> [*The question and answer at committal were tendered — the prosecutor conceded the accuracy of the transcript.*]

[8080] An example of not being able to tender the earlier statement comes from the later cross-examination of the same witness. That is because she agreed with what she had earlier said.

> [*The witness was asked about getting $20,000 from another witness.*]
>
> Did you ever say that you handed the cheque back to the police? — I don't think I was asked that question.
>
> Weren't you? — That I can recall.
>
> Were you asked this question, "Weren't you given a bank cheque for $20,000 . . . ?" Answer: "I was but I had to hand that back"? Did you give that answer? — Yes.
>
> And was that correct? — Yes.

Prior inconsistent statement turned to prior consistent statement

[8085] In some jurisdictions the old rules apply that you cannot tender the previous statement of a witness unless it is inconsistent with present evidence. We have already seen that. However, with

---

[23] The accused was a well-known businessman. He was acquitted quickly. There is no need to identify him.

a bit of skill an advocate can tender a statement as a prior inconsistent statement, then get the witness to agree with it. That way
the statement is evidence of the truth of its contents, instead of just
reflecting badly on the credit of the witness.[24] You have to pick the
occasion. The witness is not one you want to sacrifice. You want to
be able to rely on his evidence. It's not an easy thing to do. This is
how I have done it in cross-examination. Because of your preparation you know exactly what the witness has said previously. You
can put your hand instantly on any page of it. The witness does not
know that.

> Did you give evidence at the committal?
> Do you remember when that was?
> Were you asked questions?
> Many?
> Do you remember what they were?
> Did you answer each question?
> Do you remember what your answers were?
> Can't you?
> Did you ever say something on (subject)?
> Do you know if you said (quietly quoting)?
> Don't know?
> (Tender the committal evidence) You see that they kept a record of
>   what you said?
> When you gave that evidence it was soon after the event?
> You were sworn to tell the truth?
> You did?
> What you said then, now you've seen it again, was true, wasn't it?

Cutting off any escape

[8090] A cross-examiner who possesses documents will often use
them to cut off any escape of a witness. A metaphor for this technique is "closing the gates".[25] Here is a good example. In an English
case, Dr John Bodkin Adams was charged with the murder of his
patient. The patient was 81 years old. The nurses who attended
her in her last days all gave evidence. The death was in late 1950.

---

[24] *Bull v The Queen* (2000) 201 CLR 443 at 466 [79] per McHugh, Gummow and Hayne JJ.
[25] Explained in Chapter 5 [5130].

The trial was in 1957.[26] The nurses had continued working in the meantime, but they had kept notebooks about the condition of the patient and of her treatment. The nurses had not checked their notes before making statements to the police or before giving evidence. Leading counsel for the defence was Geoffrey Lawrence QC. He had the notebooks. The first witness was Nurse Stronach. He established that her earliest attempt to recall the events was some six years after the patient's death. Lawrence QC decided to lead her on before taking her to the notes.[27]

> You say that you used to give Mrs Morrell an injection of ¼ grain of morphia? — Yes, I did say so.
>
> On Dr Adams's instructions? — Yes.
>
> Are you referring to your period of day duty or night duty when you say that? — Well, night duty.
>
> Did you ever give her anything else by way of an injection? — No, I did not.
>
> No heroin? — No.
>
> No omnopon? — No.
>
> [*Now he strengthens her on the accuracy of the contemporary notes.*]
>
> I am reminded of something Miss Mason-Ellis said. I just want to ask you about it . . . "I knew what I was injecting but I cannot accurately remember now but whatever I gave was booked in a book and passed on to the next nurse"? — That was quite correct.
>
> That is quite correct? — We wrote down every injection we gave.
>
> You put down . . . ? — Yes, we kept a report of every injection we gave: this is a usual thing when you are nursing to keep a report of the injections you give.
>
> It is a usual thing? — Yes, it is the proper thing to do.
>
> Well, all experienced and trained nurses do it, do they not? — Yes, they do.
>
> And is that what you did? — Yes, indeed we did.
>
> All of you nurses did? — Yes, we all did.
>
> Was that done after each spell of duty, then, or during the night, or what? — Every time we gave an injection we wrote it down in the book; what the injection was, and the time, and signed our name.

[26] Henry Palmer, "Dr Adams' Trial for Murder" [1957] Crim LR 365–377. The jury was out for 44 minutes before returning a verdict of not guilty. Even the trial judge wrote a book about the case: Patrick Devlin, *Easing the Passing*, 1985, Bodley Head, London.

[27] Henry Palmer, "Lessons of a Cross-examination" [1957] Crim LR 773–786. It is well worth reading.

And whatever you wrote in the book would be accurate, would it not? — Oh yes.

Because it was done right at that very moment? — Yes.

In the case of these books, I suppose that everything that happened of significance in the patient's illness would also go down in the book by the nurse? — Yes.

Not only injections, I suppose, but medicines and all that sort of thing? — Yes, that is so.

. . .

And, as distinct from your memory, six years later, of course, these reports would be absolutely accurate, would they not – I mean yours would, at any rate? — Oh yes, they would be accurate for each one of us.

So that if only we had got those reports now we could see the truth of exactly what happened night by night and day by day that you were there, could we not? — Yes, but you have our word for it.

[*At last he produces the book.*]

I want you to look at that book please. [*same handed*] Would you look at the day report for the 4th June 1950 . . .

There is no doubt about it, is there, Miss Stronach that is the very book of daily and nightly records kept by nurses when you started your first spell of duty in June 1950? — Yes, that is so.

. . .

We have already seen your entries for the nights in June. Now let us see what you put in the day only a month before she died: "4 pm. Asked for bedpan. Same not used. Position changed. Patient became restless and picking bedclothes." Do you see what follows? Is this in your writing: "Hypo injection omnopon $^2/_3$rd given at 4.30 pm"? — Yes.

That means you gave that injection, does it not? — It does.

And it is an injection of omnopon? — Yes.

Now, Miss Stronach, do not think that I am blaming you for this . . . — No.

. . . but do you remember telling me this morning before you saw these contemporary records that you had never given any injection except morphia? — Well, I believed that to be true.

Well, this entry shows that your memory was playing you a trick, does it not? — Apparently so.

Obviously so. Miss Stronach, may I ask you to face this squarely. Obviously your memory played you a trick, did it not, when you said you had never injected anything but morphia? — Yes. Of course you have got to remember it is a long time ago for us to remember these things.

Summary

[8095] This is the essence of the rules on cross-examination on documents:

1. The basic common law rule from *Queen's Case* is that a witness cannot be asked questions about the contents of a document unless it is first shown to the witness and put into evidence as part of the cross-examiner's case.[28]
2. The harshness of *Queen's Case* was eased by the *Evidence Acts*.[29]
3. A witness may be cross-examined about a previous written statement or evidence without the document being shown to the witness. There is no obligation to tender.[30]
4. The document or evidence must be, by some legislation, "relative to the subject matter". "Relative" means relevant.[31] Otherwise the finality rule applies.[32]
5. Bias or corruption can be the subject of cross-examination on a document.[33]
6. The *Evidence Acts* do not make an inadmissible document admissible.[34]
7. The document must be in court or be capable of being produced.[35]
8. By the *Evidence Acts*, or by inherent or implied power, a trial judge has the discretion to require the production of a document and its tender.[36]
9. If *R v Jack* be the law, a witness cannot be handed a document and asked whether the witness still sticks to earlier evidence, unless the cross-examiner is prepared to undertake to put the document in evidence.[37]

---

[28] *Queen's Case* (1820) 2 Brod & Bing 284; 22 RR 662; 129 ER 976.

[29] Cth 1995 s. 43; Qld 1977 s. 19; WA 1906 s. 21; Tas 2001 s. 43; NT s. 20; NSW 1995 s. 43; Vic 1958 s. 36; SA 1929 s. 29; ACT 1971 s. 62.

[30] See *Evidence Acts* (above).

[31] *R v Musolino* (2003) 86 SASR 37; 139 A Crim R 488 at 51; 501 [110].

[32] *Nicholls v The Queen* (2005) 219 CLR 196 at 215–223 [37]–[56] per McHugh J.

[33] *Nicholls v The Queen* (above) at 233 [87] per McHugh J.

[34] *R v Musolino* (above) at 50; 501 [108].

[35] *R v Anderson* (1929) 21 Cr App R 178.

[36] *Alchin v Commissioner for Railways* (1935) 35 SR (NSW FC) at 509 per Jordan CJ; *Wood v Desmond* (1958) 78 WN 65 at 67; *Hrysikos v Mansfield* (2002) 5 VR 485; 135 A Crim R 179 at 505;199 [75] per Eames JA.

[37] *R v Jack* (1894) 15 LR (NSW) 196; *Alchin v Commissioner for Railways* (above) at 509; *R v Fraser* (1995) 65 SASR 269; 85 A Crim R 385 at 265–266; 390–391 per Doyle CJ;

10. A witness can be cross-examined about an inadmissible document, for example, of which the witness was not the author, but only asked if the witness still sticks to the evidence.[38] In this event the document must not be identified, and if the witness is not the author, the nature of the document or its contents must not be referred to.[39]

11. If the contents of a document, though not made by the witness, are within the personal knowledge of the witness, the witness can be asked to admit the contents of the document.[40] But though such questions may be asked, the witness need not answer unless the document is produced.[41]

12. Unless the witness is a party, the document can only be used "for the purpose of testing the witness's present evidence".[42]

13. If the attention of a witness is taken to the inconsistent part, and the witness refuses to acknowledge the inconsistency, the document can be tendered: *Evidence Acts*.

14. If the witness acknowledges the inconsistency, the document is not admissible.[43]

15. If a witness refreshes memory from part of a document, counsel can cross-examine on that part without fear. If the cross-examination is on other parts, the cross-examiner may be required to tender the document.[44]

16. Opposing counsel can require the tender of the document during cross-examination,[45] and possibly at any time before the end of the case.[46]

J Boag and Son Brewing Ltd v Bridon Investments Ltd (2001) 10 Tas R 26 at 33 [13] (Slicer J).

[38] *R v Orton* [1922] VLR 469 at 470 (Cussen J); *R v Bedington* [1970] Qd R 353 at 359–360; *Alister v The Queen* (1984) 154 CLR 404 at 442–443 per Wilson and Dawson JJ.

[39] *R v Seham Yousry* (1914) 11 Cr App R 13 at 18; *R v Orton* (above) and *Alister v The Queen* (above); *R v Trotter* (1982) 7 A Crim R 8 at 22 (Vic CCA).

[40] *Alchin v Commissioner for Railways* (above); *R v Cooper* (1985) 82 Cr App R 74 at 78–79.

[41] *R v Banks* (1916) 12 Cr App R 74 at 75–76.

[42] *Alchin v Commissioner of Railways* (above).

[43] *R v Soma* (2003) 212 CLR 299 at 317 [57] per McHugh J.

[44] *Senat v Senat* [1965] P 172; *R v Harrison* [1966] VR 72 at 75–76; *Hrysikos v Mansfield* (above) at 505; 199 [75].

[45] *Hatziparadissis v GFC Manufacturing Co* [1978] VR 181 at 183 (Harris J); *R v Trotter* (above) at 19.

[46] *R v Foggo; Ex parte Attorney-General* [1989] 2 Qd R 49; *Alexander v Manley* (2004) 29 WAR 194.

17. Cross-examination by counsel on parts of a privileged document that counsel has in possession may waive privilege of the whole document.[47] But such a waiver depends on the circumstances.[48]

---

[47] *Burnell v British Transport Commission* [1956] 1 QB 187 at 190.
[48] *Attorney-General (NT) v Maurice* (1986) 161 CLR 475 at 497–498 per Dawson J.

Chapter 9

Re-examination

The nature of re-examination

[9000] After cross-examination has ended, you can ask further question of your witness. This is re-examination. Its main purpose is to remove or to explain away or to qualify the damage done to the evidence in cross-examination. If the damage were not explained or at least qualified, there would be prejudice to the party's case or discredit to the witness. More particularly, re-examination is designed to repair any distortion or incomplete account or ambiguity that cross-examination has produced.[1] If there has been no cross-examination there cannot be re-examination.

[9005] The aims of re-examination are:

1. To remove ambiguities or uncertainties.
2. To restore facts in issue.
3. To revive the credit of the witness.

Is it necessary?

[9010] Re-examination is one of the hardest of the advocate's tasks. Unlike examination-in-chief and cross-examination it cannot be planned. The ill-advised re-examination can bring your case horribly unstuck. In cross-examination the first decision to make is whether it is necessary. The same applies to re-examination. You will have taken instructions as fully as possible. You will have watched your witness closely during your opponent's cross-examination. You must make a decision in the running on whether you should re-examine.

---

[1] Summed up in *R v AJS* (2005) 159 A Crim R 327 at 341 [48] (Vic CA).

[9015] The factors you will take into account are these:

1. Has cross-examination damaged your party's case either on the facts or on the credit of your witness? If not, no re-examination is necessary.
2. Are there ambiguities that need to be explained?
3. If your case is damaged, can you diffuse it? If you don't know how, and you re-examine, the damage may be increased.

Riley J described a re-examination in which you have no idea why a witness gave such evidence in cross-examination: "You would bear the substantial risk that that things will go from terrible to devastating."[2] One way around that difficulty may be the rare case in which a trial judge will allow you to take instructions from your party before you start your re-examination.[3]

[9020] Here is an example of a re-examination which foundered. Quentin Tipungwuti's case is referred to in cross-examination.[4] Regis Pangaraminni said in cross-examination that he was told of the wounds to the deceased, and passed them on to the Aboriginal community. That cross-examination was designed to undermine Quentin's later confession to the police describing the wounds. The prosecutor did not diffuse the effect of the cross-examination. He aggravated it by asking the witness what the police had told the witness about the wounds.

> What did he tell you then? — He just told me that the deceased got stabbed and . . .
> Did he tell you how many times the deceased got stabbed? — Yes.
> How many times did he tell you? — Four, I think.
> Did he tell you where those stabs were? — Yes, he showed me.
> How did he show you? — One at the back, one down the throat, down the side and one on the belly (demonstrating).[5]

---

[2] Justice Riley, *The Little Red Book of Advocacy*, 2003, Law Society of the Northern Territory, p. 57.

[3] It was allowed by the trial judge in *R v Santos and Carrion* (1987) 45 SASR 556; 26 A Crim R 432 at 564; 441.

[4] See Chapter 6 [6065]. See cross-examination of the expert in Chapter 7 [7085].

[5] *R v Tipungwuti* (Northern Territory Supreme Court) 1 August 1989, before Rice J and jury.

Arising from cross-examination

[9025] The re-examination must arise from the cross-examination. Here is an example. Daniel Fitzgibbon was seriously injured when he went head first into shallow water and his head hit the sandy bottom. It happened after a yacht race in Sydney. The winner had been thrown in. Mr Fitzgibbon said he was nudged and could not keep his footing. The cross-examination was to the effect that he had chosen to dive in and his injuries were his own fault. Dennis Wheelahan QC was counsel for Mr Fitzgibbon. Here is part of the re-examination. Notice the one issue in each question. Every one of them is non-leading. Their effect is enhanced by their shortness.

> Did you have any intention of entering the water that night? — None at all.
> Did you know how high the deck was from the water? — I had not been to the yacht club before so I wasn't aware of the heights of anything.
> Did you know how deep the water was above the sandy beach? — Yeah, I had no idea of the surroundings.
> Did you know what the nature of the bottom was? — No, I'd never been to the yacht club before.
> Did you know it was sand? — No.
> Or rock? — I didn't know anything.[6]

[9030] Here is the re-examination of Mr W.A. Cadbury by Rufus Isaacs after Carson's slashing cross-examination:[7]

> Has your ceasing to buy San Thomé cocoa in 1908 had any effect on the output or consumption of cocoa from there? — No, not on the conditions of native labour.
> In order to do anything effective about those conditions what view have you always taken? — That it was necessary to have the combination of the other chocolate manufacturers: that alone we could do nothing to ameliorate the conditions.
> Did you take any steps to that end? — We attempted to get the American manufacturers to join us in our action but without success.
> Has the action you have taken by ceasing to purchase cocoa from the islands had any effect on your profits? — None at all.[8]

---

[6] *The Waterways Authority v Fitzgibbon* (2005) 79 ALJR 1816 at 1838–1839; 221 ALR 402 at 433 [150].

[7] Set out in Chapter 6 [6050]. The Cadbury case is unreported. The latest discussion of it is to be found in Lowell J Satre, *Chocolate on Trial: Slavery, Politics and the Ethics of Business*, 2005, Ohio University Press, pp. 149–82.

[8] Rufus Isaacs (1860–1930) became Marquess of Reading. He was appointed Lord Chief Justice in 1913 (as Reading LCJ).

[9035] I did say that re-examination must arise from cross-examination. It must not be used to bring out evidence that ought to have been elicited in examination-in-chief.[9]

No leading questions

[9040] The rule is that you cannot ask a leading question in re-examination, although in special circumstances a judge can allow it.[10] When we looked at the nature of leading questions we noted that it was permissible to direct a witness to a topic. This aspect of directing a witness is never so important as in re-examination. A frequent method is to repeat what was said in cross-examination and then ask a non-leading question on the topic.

[9045] In this example, Brian Martin[11] was re-examining:

> You agreed with Mr Borick yesterday after refreshing your memory that in the Magistrates' Court you looked at the accused and said "The person in the box there could be the person but the hair is different" . . . What did you mean by the expression "could be the person"? — I meant it was the person.
> Why did you use the expression "could be"? — I was being cautious.[12]

Here is another example:

> Where you said this morning in relation to K46 which was Mr Blackett's draft of the minutes of the 11 August board meeting? — Yes, may I look?
> Certainly? — Yes.
> You said in an answer this morning that you thought that that draft was wrong? — Well, as a matter of semantics.
> When you say "a matter of semantics", what do you mean by that? — (answer given).[13]

As you can also see from the last question in each of these examples, the advocate asked the witness what was meant by some word or

---

[9] *R v AJS* (2005) 159 A Crim R 327 at 342 [50] (Vic CA).

[10] *Rawcliffe v The Queen* (2000) 22 WAR 490; 115 A Crim R 509.

[11] Later Martin J (Supreme Court of South Australia) then B R Martin CJ (Supreme Court of Northern Territory).

[12] *R v Szach* (1980) 23 SASR 504; 2 A Crim R 321 (CCA) per King CJ at 567–568; 327–328.

[13] *Whitlam v ASIC* (2003) 199 ALR 674 at 723 [100]. [This part is not in the report of the case (2003) 57 NSWLR 559.]

phrase in the earlier answer. This is designed to remove any possible ambiguity from the evidence.

[9050] The re-examination can direct the witness to a complete topic. In *R v Fish and Swan*, a witness had said in cross-examination that he had no recollection of violence by the police in the office. The re-examination was as follows:

> Sir, you made reference when you were being asked questions . . . about Ms Fish and the area of the office? — Yes.
>
> You made reference to the fact that you had no clear recollection of what Ms Fish did on this night, now apart from the office area, do you have any recollection as to what she did that night? — She was one of the people lined up at the back of the police van with the baton. She was the one that identified me as one of the group.[14]

Explaining the reason

[9055] Often a re-examination will explain a reason for the actions of the witness. In the following example, the victim of a sexual assault was a young girl when the events occurred. The place was the flat of the accused, which he shared with his wife [VM] and young son. The case was heard some 20 years later. The witness was profoundly deaf and gave evidence through a signing interpreter. In cross-examination she had admitted that VM was present in the flat at all times, but she had made no complaint. Nor did she complain to her mother. The re-examination was designed to reduce or remove the effects of failure to complain.

> Why didn't you go straight to VM and complain to her? — Because he had threatened. He had gestured to me the cut throat gesture and told me to "shush" putting his index finger over his mouth and also because I was afraid my mother would smack me because – and that's why I just didn't say anything to anybody.
>
> Before he made that gesture about cutting your throat, do you recall the occasions when you say the accused did things to you? — Yes.
>
> Why didn't you tell VM? — I was afraid. I was a young child.
>
> Why didn't you tell your mother about any of these things? — I didn't want to.
>
> Why? — My mother would smack me; she smacked me often.[15]

---

[14] *R v Fish and Swan* (2002) 131 A Crim R 172 at 187 [73]. For some of the cross-examination see Chapter 6 [6075].

[15] *R v Markulesi* (2001) 52 NSWLR 82; 125 A Crim R 186 (CCA) at 117; 219 [155].

[9060] Here is an arch example where re-examination shows the reasons for the actions of the witness. Cross-examining counsel had the witness agree that she had rung the police to say that she did not want to proceed with her allegation. She said she did this because she was scared. Here is the re-examination:

> Why were you scared? — I was scared that if I went through with like going to court and everything what might happen to my children and then —
> What did you think might happen to your children? — In some cases like this I didn't want them to die, you know, I was just scared for their lives.
> And what had made you scared? — Just that I had heard that he was not a very nice person in that sort of area and that he already would have a friend of his to basically come through with a rifle and kill us all, basically.[16]

Rebutting recent invention

[9065] The cross-examiner might ask a witness if the evidence had been recently invented. Questions that contain expressions such as "recent fabrication", "after-thought", "recent invention", and "belated concoction" all imply that the evidence has been made up at some time just before giving evidence. It does not matter whether the suggestion is put in one straightforward question or in a round-about way. If recent invention is alleged in cross-examination it can be rebutted in re-examination.[17]

[9070] Other examples of questions in cross-examination which allege recent invention are:

> You're not making this up as well, as you go, are you?[18]

and

> You've changed your story to make it a bit easier on yourself.[19]

[9075] The introduction of the earlier statement rebuts the allega-tion of concoction. If the earlier statement is spoken, there is no

---

16 *Marlowe v The Queen* (2000) 113 A Crim R 118 at 122 [14] (Tas CCA). By majority the court found the re-examination did not introduce undue prejudice.
17 *Nominal Defendant v Clements* (1960) 104 CLR 476 at 488 and 493.
18 *R v Fraser* (1995) 65 SASR 260; 85 A Crim R 385.
19 *R v Smith* (No 2) (1995) 64 SASR 1; 80 A Crim R 491 at 36; 525.

question of hearsay involved, for its purpose is simply to rebut the allegation.[20] If the earlier statement is written you can tender it. But if you want to re-examine to introduce a prior consistent statement, you must make sure that the witness confirms that the prior consistent statement is true.[21]

Reviving credit

[9080] One of the purposes of re-examination is to revive the credit of the witness, which may have been damaged in cross-examination.

[9085] An example of reviving credit is in *R v Ready and Manning*. A prosecution witness had made a statement to the police. Counsel for the accused had cross-examined her about some of the things she had told the police at the time she made the statement. Counsel suggested that the detectives had said she would get an indemnity if she did make the statement. In re-examination the prosecutor asked about the statement and then:

> Is that the same as you have told us here today? — As far as possible, yes.
>
> Had anything been suggested about an indemnity up to then? — No, it occurred just at the end, after I had given my statement.[22]

Re-examining on documents

[9090] If a witness is cross-examined on part of a document, the re-examiner may prove that particular part of the document, together with such other parts of the document that explain or modify it.[23]

Summary

[9095] In summary, these are my recommendations:

1. No leading questions.
2. Issues must arise from cross-examination.
3. No new matters except by leave.

---

[20] *R v Georgiev* (2001) 119 A Crim R 363 at 378 [44] (Vic CA).

[21] *R v AJS* (2005) 159 A Crim R 327 at 342 [51] (Vic CA).

[22] *R v Ready and Manning* [1942] VLR 85 at 94.

[23] *Meredith v Innes* (1931) 31 SR (NSW) 104 (FC – 5 member court) at 112 per Street CJ; *R v Titijewski* [1970] VR 371 at 375, 378 (CCA); *R v Kehagias* [1985] VR 107 at 118–119 (CCA).

4. Explain expressions used by the witness in cross-examination.
5. Explain motives or reasons.
6. Explain the whole of an event or incident.
7. Restore credit or mitigate discredit.
8. Give the whole of a conversation with a central party.
9. Use the whole of a statement to explain a prior inconsistency.
10. Try to finish on a good answer.

Chapter 10

Admissibility, objections and submissions

Admissibility

[10000] Evidence is relevant and admissible if it increases or diminishes the probability of the existence of a fact in issue or of a fact behind a fact in issue.[1] The adjectives used to describe such evidence are "relevant" and "probative". Irrelevant evidence is inadmissible.[2]

[10005] Relevant evidence will not be received by a court:

1. If its reception is forbidden by law.
2. If there is an accepted objection such as public interest immunity or legal professional privilege.[3]
3. If its prejudicial effect outweighs its probative value.[4]
4. If the probative value is so low as not to justify the time convenience and cost of its proof.[5]
5. If the bad conduct of an opponent's witness makes the reception contrary to public policy such as the police acting improperly to induce a confession.[6]

[10010] The test that a court uses to decide admissibility is not some form of mathematical calculation. As we know, judges are human beings. Of course, mathematicians are human beings too,

---

[1] *Director of Public Prosecutions v Kilbourne* [1973] AC 729 at 757 per Lord Simon.

[2] *Smith v The Queen* (2001) 206 CLR 650 at 653–654 [6]–[7].

[3] *Carter v Northmore Hale Davy and Leake* (1995) 183 CLR 121.

[4] Often called the Christie discretion from *R v Christie* [1914] AC 545. In *R v Sang* [1980] AC 402 at 454 Lord Scarman said that *R v Christie* is "only a staging post in the development of the law" on discretion.

[5] *Palmer v The Queen* (1998) 193 CLR 1 per McHugh J at 24 [55]; *Nicholls v The Queen* (2005) 219 CLR 196 at 223 [56] per McHugh J.

[6] For example *R v Anderson* (1991) 1 NTLR 149 (Martin J); See also *Hawkins v The Queen* (1994) 181 CLR 440; *R v Mason* [1988] 1 WLR 139. See generally Andrew Palmer, *Proof*, 2003, Lawbook Co, Sydney, Chapter 8 "Analysing for admissibility".

but mathematics is not based on human affairs and court cases are. The complex events in a court case make it difficult for an advocate to arrive at a clear formulation of the standard for admissibility. Even if that formulation could be made, assessing how it would apply in a given case is no easy task. The reason for the difficulty is that the test for relevance is "logic and experience".[7]

[10015] In *R v Matthews* Schreiner JA said:

> Relevancy is based upon a blend of logic and experience lying outside the law. The law starts with this practical or commonsense relevancy and then adds material to it or, more commonly, excludes material from it, the resultant being what is legally relevant and therefore admissible.[8]

"Logic and experience", as Schreiner JA said, is commonly the test for exclusion of evidence. Put more accurately, although logic is the test of relevance, not all evidence that is logically relevant is legally admissible.[9] For example, prejudicial evidence may be excluded where neither logic nor experience shows it pointing to the guilt of the accused.[10]

[10020] Logic is not deductive logic. Admissibility is therefore a matter of degree.[11] It is no wonder, then, that an appeal can turn on whether a judge has properly used "experience and common sense".[12]

Facts in issue

[10025] This chapter began with defining relevance by reference to a fact in issue. The ultimate issues in any case are the elements of the cause of action in a civil case, or the elements of the offence in a criminal case. Thus there will be issues about the facts that constitute those elements. Behind those facts are further facts. Evidence is also

---

[7] *Director of Public Prosecutions v Kilbourne* [1973] AC 729 at 756 per Lord Simon; *Hoch v The Queen* (1988) 165 CLR 292 at 297.

[8] *R v Matthews* [1960] 1 SA 752 (Appellate Division) at 758 per Schreiner JA. Approved (but wrongly cited): *R v Harmer* (1985) 28 A Crim R 35 at 41; *R v Fraser* (1995) 65 SASR 260 at 267.

[9] *R v Stephenson* [1976] VR 376 at 380 (CCA).

[10] *Pfennig v The Queen* (1995) 182 CLR 461 at 482.

[11] *Sutton v The Queen* (1984) 152 CLR 528 at 564–565 per Dawson J.

[12] *DPP v Boardman* [1975] AC 421 (HL) at 444–445 per Lord Wilberforce.

admissible if it tends to prove or disprove a fact relevant to a fact in issue.

> A fact is relevant to another fact when it is so related to that fact that, according to the ordinary course of events, either by itself or in connection with other facts, it proves or makes probable the past, present or future existence or non-existence of the other fact.[13]

[10030] It is worth noting that there is no distinction in relevance between the evidence a witness gives and whether the witness is believable. As McHugh J said, "The credibility of evidence is locked to the credibility of its deponent."[14]

[10035] These extracts from the case law show the difficulty faced by every advocate in trying to resolve whether a given piece of evidence is relevant. Whether you act for a plaintiff or for the prosecution you must make that judgment. Your decision determines which witnesses will give evidence on which subjects. If you act for the defence you must decide whether to object to any evidence because of irrelevance or because of prejudice. If the case against the defence is proved to the necessary degree, you must decide whether to lead evidence. If you act for the defence and you do lead evidence, the positions of the advocates are then reversed.

Proof

[10040] The standard of proof in civil cases has been long settled. It is clear enough that the plaintiff must prove its case on the balance of probabilities and has the duty to lead evidence to prove it. In application there is much debate. For example, courts now say that a property owner must not be negligent – never mind the status of the entrant.[15] Still, it must be proof and not conjecture, suspicion or possibility.[16] A defendant in a civil case will sometimes have the evidential and legal burden. So in a contract case a defendant might allege misrepresentation. If so, the defendant must prove it. If the defendant admits borrowing the money but says he paid it back, he has to prove it.

[10045] In a criminal case the prosecution must prove the guilt of the accused beyond reasonable doubt.

---

[13] *Goldsmith v Sandilands* (2002) 76 ALJR 1024 at 1029–1939 [31] per McHugh J.
[14] *Palmer v The Queen* (1998) 193 CLR 1 at 24 [56] per McHugh J.
[15] *Australian Safeway Stores Pty Ltd v Zaluzna* (1987) 162 CLR 479.
[16] See generally Andrew Palmer, *Proof*, 2003, Lawbook Co, Sydney.

Throughout the web of the English criminal law one golden thread is always to be seen — that it is the duty of the prosecution to prove the prisoner's guilt . . . If, at the end of and on the whole of the case, there is reasonable doubt, created by the evidence given by the prosecution or the prisoner . . . the prosecution has not made out its case and the prisoner is entitled to an acquittal.[17]

[10050] In many criminal cases there is simply a denial of the involvement that the prosecution alleges. In one case it will be "I was not there". In another case it will be "Yes, I was there but only as an onlooker". But some cases have aspects that arise only from the defence. Examples are provocation, self-defence and duress. Belief in consent on a charge of rape is another.[18] Quite often there is evidence of intoxication by alcohol or another drug or a combination of them. Various mental states are other defences.

[10055] The evidence on these so-called defences generally emerges from the defence advocate's cross-examination of prosecution witnesses. By the end of all the evidence, the defence advocate must be able to point to evidence from which one or more of these defences may be inferred.

[10060] These defences must have some basis. They cannot be speculation or fanciful theory. When such a defence arises from the evidence, the prosecution must disprove it beyond reasonable doubt, or fail.[19] At the end of the case there is often lively debate between advocates and judge on whether there is sufficient evidence to raise the defence. The resolution of that issue by the judge determines whether the jury is to be given a direction about that defence. It is obvious that in cases where these defences arise, the responsibilities on the opposing advocates are significant. The defence advocate hopes to raise the issue, and if it is raised the prosecutor tries to negate it.[20] The aim is the favourable direction of the judge, and the prize is the jury verdict.

---

[17] *Woolmington v Director of Public Prosecutions* [1935] AC 462 at 481 per Lord Sankey.

[18] *Director of Public Prosecutions (NT) v WJI* (2004) 219 CLR 43; *R v Saragozza* [1984] VR 118; *R v Morgan* [1976] AC 182.

[19] *R v Abusafiah* (1991) 24 NSWLR 531 at 541 (CCA).

[20] But as Lord Sumner said in *Thompson v The King* [1918] AC 221 at 232: "The prosecution cannot credit the defence with fancy defences in order to rebut them at the outset with some damning piece of prejudice."

Circumstantial cases

[10065] Circumstantial cases are based on direct evidence and inferences. They are often more powerful than cases that rely wholly on direct evidence. A circumstantial case was described by Wigmore as being either like links in a chain or like strands in a cable.[21] Another simile is that a circumstantial case is like a jigsaw puzzle.[22] These cases tantalise the advocates because of the difficulty in arguing which evidence is relevant and admissible, and which inferences can be drawn from the evidence that is admitted. Take the essence of the following two examples and consider how the arguments of the advocates would have run.

[10070] The first is *Luxton v Vines*.[23] This was the evidence in a civil negligence case where an injured man sued the representative of unknown drivers.

1. Mr Luxton was prone to blackouts.
2. One winter evening he was walking along a country road.
3. He was found beside the road with severe injuries.
4. Had he fallen, the injuries would have been different.
5. The defendant represented all the unknown drivers.

The case turned on whether the plaintiff had proved negligence. The court held that he had not proved that his injuries were caused by a motor vehicle. The plaintiff failed.

[10075] The second example is *O'Leary v The King*.[24] This was a murder case.

1. A man was found battered to death early one Sunday morning.
2. The place was a timber camp where there were not many men.
3. A group of men had drunk a lot of alcohol during the day in nearby towns on Saturday and were affected by it.
4. Mr O'Leary had savagely assaulted three men on Saturday evening without cause.
5. Mr O'Leary had threatened to assault and shoot three other men.
6. No-one else had acted in this violent way.

---

[21] Referred to by Dawson J in *Shepherd v The Queen* (1990) 170 CLR 573 at 579.

[22] *R v Handy* [2002] 2 SCR 908 at 944 [91]; 213 DLR (4th) 385; 164 CCC (3 d) 481. See also *De Gruchy v The Queen* (2002) 211 CLR 85 at 95 [48] per Kirby J.

[23] *Luxton v Vines* (1952) 85 CLR 352.

[24] *O'Leary v The King* (1946) 73 CLR 566.

The issue was who was the killer. The defence objected to the evidence on points 4 and 5 without success.

Objections
Objections to evidence

[10080] When you object to evidence that you argue should not be admitted, you should base your submission on the absence of relevance of the evidence, or that it should not be admitted for the reasons set out above in [10005].

[10085] Occasionally you will make the difficult tactical decision not to object to inadmissible evidence. You will be conscious of the effect that your objection will have on the fact-finder. Some of the reasons not to object are these. The evidence may have little probative force and you may not want to give the impression that you are finding fault with trifles or being obstructive. Perhaps the evidence will be properly proved by your opponent later. Often you will base your decision on the atmosphere you want to create or at least not dispel. Of course you will not object to inadmissible evidence that suits your case.

[10090] In your objection you should adopt the following procedure. If the exclusion of the evidence would result in the complete end to your opponent's case, you should make the objection before the trial starts. If the excluded evidence would only reduce the force of the opponent's case, ask your opponent not to refer to that evidence in the opening address. The formal hearing of the objection takes place just before your opponent calls that evidence. It is wise to mention the intended objection to the judge in advance. Depending on the length of argument, the judge's own affairs may need some adjustment. If there is a jury, the judge may want to hear the objection before the jury is empanelled or when they are due for discharge for the evening. Try to work out how long the argument will take. There may have to be witnesses called on *voir dire* or on a *Basha* inquiry,[25] and that will lengthen the procedure.

[10095] The *voir dire* is the hearing of witnesses before judge alone. One example in a criminal case is where you submit that a confession

---

[25] *R v Basha* (1989) 39 A Crim R 337.

is not voluntary. The principles in a *voir dire* for that purpose are well known[26] and the hearing may take quite a long time.[27] Another reason for a *voir dire* in a criminal case may be when you submit that the witnesses might have concocted a story against the accused.[28]

[10100] Where you wish to exclude evidence and your argument is based only on statements and depositions, this is not a *voir dire* because there is no witness to give evidence. It is a submission.

[10105] A *Basha* inquiry is not a *voir dire*.[29] It is designed to allow a defence advocate in a criminal case to cross-examine a witness who could not give evidence at committal. The prime example is a co-accused who pleads guilty and is sentenced on the basis of being prepared to give evidence against the accused.

[10110] Whatever form your objection takes, it must be made, and made no later than when your opponent seeks to introduce the evidence.[30] You must identify clearly and precisely the evidence you object to and be prepared to give the same detail in your reasons for your objection.[31] If you do not make an objection it will be very hard to persuade an appeal court that the evidence was wrongly given. As Viscount Simon said:

> It is not a proper use of counsel's discretion to raise no objection at the time in order to preserve a ground of objection for a possible appeal.[32]

This remark has been approved and applied many times.[33] Other courts have said similar things. Fullagar J cautioned against two bites of the cherry.[34]

---

[26] *Ajodha v The State* [1982] AC 204 at 221–222 (PC). Approved: *MacPherson v The Queen* (1981) 147 CLR 512.

[27] Examples of these are *R v Banner* [1970] VR 240 where the *voir dire* took 10 days; *R v Anderson* (1991) 1 NTLR 149; 57 A Crim R 143 (one day) (see Chapter 6 [6035]).

[28] *DPP v Kilbourne* [1973] AC 729 where the trial judge excluded "intra-group" evidence. See also *Hoch v The Queen* (1988) 165 CLR 292.

[29] *R v Sandford* (1994) 37 NSWLR 172.

[30] *Woods v Rogers; Ex parte Woods* [1983] 2 Qd R 212; (1983) 9 A Crim R 209 (CA).

[31] Heydon J "Reciprocal duties of Bench and Bar" (2007) 81 ALJ 23 at 27–28.

[32] *Stirland v Director of Public Prosecutions* [1944] AC 315 at 328.

[33] Examples are *R v Donald* (1983) 34 SASR 10 at 25 (CCA); *Brian Gardner Motors Pty Ltd v Bembridge* (2000) 120 A Crim R 53 at 61 [52] (WA, Hasluck J).

[34] *R v Koutsouridis* (1982) 7 A Crim R 237 at 242 (Vic CCA).

Objections to forms of questions

[10115] An advocate will object to questions in evidence-in-chief for the following main reasons:

1. The question is leading: "You went across the road then, didn't you?"
2. It assumes unprovable facts in the case. The objectionable questions often begin "Do you recall . . ." or similar.
3. There is more than one issue in the question.
4. The questioner interrupts the answer.
5. The question contains an incorrect paraphrase of earlier evidence.

[10120] In a jury case the advocate who objects might ask for the jury to retire. That course is advisable if the objection will take some time or if it will raise some sensitive matter. The request is simply made.

> Your Honour, I object to this question. It is a decision for you alone because it is a matter of law. The argument may take some time. There is no need to keep the jury in here for that.

[10125] An advocate may object to questions asked by an opponent who is cross-examining. Of course there can be no objection that a question is leading, for it is an accepted technique in cross-examination to ask leading questions.

[10130] The form of the objection will be as follows:

> Your Honour, I object to the question.

Usually you will then wait. If the question in examination-in-chief is obviously leading, the judge will often say so to the advocate asking the questions. Otherwise you will add:

> The question is a leading one.

OR

> There is more than one issue to the question.

Where the objection is a little more detailed, you will have to provide those details.

Submissions

Unfair hearing or abuse of process

[10135] The judge will stop a case if the trial cannot be fair.[35] If the action is an abuse of process it will be stopped.[36] If the case suggests that either of these grounds exists, you should raise the matter with the judge as a preliminary issue and before the hearing proper is due to begin. Generally your application will be for the plaintiff's case to be struck out, or in a criminal case for there to be a permanent stay. The judge and court officials like to have advance notice of this sort of submission so they can arrange their affairs accordingly. They may hold off summoning a jury at least until the judge decides on the submission.

No case to answer

[10140] The submission of "no case to answer" is a legal submission. It is made by the defence at the end of the opponent's case – whether plaintiff in a civil case or prosecution in a criminal case. The submission is made to the judge alone and in the absence of a jury. The submission is simply that the elements of the cause of action or of the criminal charge have not been supported by evidence. There is a fundamental flaw in the case. To take some obvious examples, the plaintiff who claims damages for injuries because of the defendant's bad driving of a motor vehicle may fail to prove that the defendant was the driver. In a criminal case alleging incest, the prosecution fails to prove that the alleged victim was the child of the accused.[37]

[10145] In a civil case, at the end of the plaintiff's evidence the defence can submit that there is no case to answer. You must be sure that the plaintiff's case has not been made out at all because you will be put to your election. This means that you must elect to make the no case submission or to answer the plaintiff's case. You cannot do both.

[10150] In a criminal case, you will not be put to your election if you make a no case submission at the end of the prosecution evidence. You can be confident of one thing, and that is that the prosecution

---

[35] *Dietrich v The Queen* (1992) 177 CLR 292 at 311.
[36] *Williams v Spautz* (1992) 174 CLR 509.
[37] *R v Umanski* [1961] VR 242.

has led all of the evidence it can. The prosecution is not allowed to split its case and perhaps leave a little to use in cross-examination of any witnesses who may be called by the defence.[38]

Submissions at the end of the case

[10155] Before final addresses to a jury, the trial judge will usually invite submissions from the advocates. The reason for this invitation is to isolate the evidence that attracts the law, and to settle the law that applies to the evidence as isolated. If you are well prepared you will have long since planned for this. Your conduct of the whole case will have been designed to have the evidence in the state you want by the time the case finishes. The evidence will attract the law as you determined in your preparation. You see the two parts, the evidence and the law, sometimes as a pair or a couplet, and sometimes as the one being. One cannot exist without the other. Perhaps a better description is a symbiosis. The evidence will attract legal conclusions. As advocate you argue them both.

Legal submissions generally

[10160] Legal submissions are based on statute and the decisions of other courts of authority. With experience you will develop a certain style in your legal submissions. Generally the authorities you cite in your favour will contain statements of principle rather than just sets of facts that are similar to those of the present case. Always cite the authorised reports, that is, those approved by the judges.[39] Refer to the authorities both for and against your position. Technically and ethically it is the correct thing to do. Tactically it is an excellent scheme. You distinguish the contrary authorities or show that they should be confined to their own facts. Perhaps, to use Pope's expression, you will damn them with faint praise.[40] By the time your opponent refers to those authorities they will seem to lack force.

[10165] There is another way of making submissions, not often seen but one of the most effective. In this method you begin by talking indirectly about your subject. The authorities you hand the judge

---

[38] *R v Chin* (1985) 157 CLR 671; *R v Soma* (2003) 212 CLR 299.
[39] See Chapter 14 [14175]–[14195].
[40] Alexander Pope "An Epistle to Dr Arbuthnot", 1735, line 201.

are the right ones but the passages you quote are not quite the ones that advance your position as well as possible. The judge will then pick up the argument and refer to the best parts of the judgments. It is the judge who shows how correct the point is by taking counsel to the relevant parts of the evidence. All this will take great panache on your part to allow the judge to lead and refine your arguments. The judge's point is always the best point.

[10170] There are some demanding cases where the submissions will be difficult. Perhaps not all the authorities go your way, or the evidence on which you rely is ambiguous. You may be able to persuade the judge but it will not be easy. In this sort of case, you can follow the lead of the best advocates and frankly acknowledge the obstacles in your way. With careful advocacy you may be able to induce the judge to find the solution for you. The judge who is apt to pick holes in an advocate's argument is just the one who will pick holes in the difficulty you point to in finding the answer. Now that's class.

Recommendations on a no case submission

[10175] These are my recommendations on a no case submission:

1. Analyse the elements of the main charge or cause.
2. Analyse the elements of any alternative charge or cause.
3. Collect all the direct evidence on each element.
4. Collect all the circumstantial evidence on each element.
5. Is there an absence of direct evidence on any element?
6. Does any circumstantial evidence exclude all hypotheses consistent with your opponent's case?
7. Is all the evidence incapable of proving any element?
8. Take the court to the elements.
9. Take the court to the evidence.
10. Refer to any authorities.

Chapter 11

The addresses

Addresses generally

[11000] Generations of advocates have found that a good address, opening and closing, has these parts:

1. Introduction.
2. Identification of the issues.
3. Evidence that proves each issue.
4. Conclusions or inferences to be drawn.

In its composition, it should be logical and expressed in simple language.

[11005] In a jury case it is generally not wise to refer to the law in any detail. The reasons are these. If you do refer to the law you must do it by way of submission as you would to a judge. Most advocates find that ungainly. The judge will be referring to the law in the directions to the jury. Those directions of law will be combined with the evidence you have referred to and your arguments or submissions contained in your final address. You will often have to refer to some general law, but try to make it so well known as not to need citation or submission. It will possibly take the following form:

> The prosecution has to prove beyond reasonable doubt that when he fired the shot Mr Black intended to kill Mr Gray or cause him really serious bodily injury. I expect that his Honour will tell you that when he directs you on the law. Either he will reinforce what I said, or correct me if I am wrong.

[11010] There are several things that you must not do in any address. You must not give your opinion, except perhaps on matters of general human nature. You must address truly and not mislead the

court. You must not refer to a fact or allegation not in evidence. In your final address you must not be overly provocative, especially if you are prosecuting. As the Privy Council advised:

> There is an obvious difference between a robust speech and one which is xenophobic, inflammatory and seeks to make use of inadmissible and irrelevant material.[1]

[11015] Consider the description of a final address by Shane Herbert QC. He invariably appeared for the defence, but the fine qualities of his speech apply to all addresses.

> He was witty but not funny; thorough but not long winded; above all else, clear and direct . . . He reduced the issues to clear and straightforward propositions.[2]

Opening address

[11020] The opening address sets out what the case is about. Pitch the opening at a conservative level. If the evidence emerges more strongly than you have opened, that is to your advantage. If you open it too high and the evidence does not reach that level, the defence will take advantage of the chance for comment in final address.

Civil cases

[11025] In a civil case before a judge sitting alone, the pleadings and a good many other documents will be on the court file. Most judges read all of those documents before the case starts. You can generally assume that the judge knows at least the essence of the case before the formal start.

[11030] In a case of any complexity, aim to use some of the charts you have prepared. A chronology and a chart of financial transactions, where relevant, are often the most informative. Make sure you give the defence a copy well beforehand.

Criminal cases

[11035] A criminal case before a jury calls for an opening address that will explain the prosecution case. You must take care not to

---

[1] *Benedetto v The Queen* [2003] 1 WLR 1545 at 1566 [55].
[2] Obituary (1995) 69 ALJ 1016.

suggest that the defence can make an answer. The right to silence still exists in the criminal law.

[11040] The opening address in a straightforward case is generally fairly short. A prosecutor will try to speak for not more than an hour. In delivery it should be quite low key. An appeal to emotions might be a characteristic of the final address but not of the opening. There is a simple reason for this absence of emotion. The early prosecution witnesses may be photographers who will take the jury through each of their photos, and the crime scene examiners who will give evidence of what they saw and collected. An opening with emotion would fall very flat with that type of evidence to follow.

[11045] Start with a short account of what the case is about. An example is the opening of Christmas Humphreys, the leading prosecutor in a joint murder case before Lord Goddard and a jury. After some short formal matters, Mr Humphreys said:

> The case for the prosecution is this: that Craig deliberately and wilfully murdered that police constable, and thereafter gloried in the murder; that Bentley incited Craig to begin the shooting and, although technically under arrest at the actual time of the killing of Miles, was party to that murder and equally responsible in law.[3]

[11050] Another excellent example of the introduction comes from the *Chamberlain* case. Mrs Chamberlain was supposed to have cut her baby's throat, without motive. Mr Chamberlain was alleged to have hidden the body. The case was celebrated. There had been two inquests. Mrs Chamberlain had told people that a dingo had taken her baby. She gave sworn evidence of that at both inquests. The media could not leave it alone. The murder trial began in September 1982 before Muirhead J and a jury. Ian Barker QC prosecuted. This is how his opening address started. Note the chilling last sentence.

> A baby was killed at Ayers Rock on 17 August 1980, during the evening, between eight and nine o'clock. It was Sunday. The child was then just under ten weeks old, having been born on 11 June. She was called Azaria Chamberlain, and was the daughter of the accused Michael Leigh Chamberlain and Alice Lynne Chamberlain. The body of the child was never found but, having heard the evidence concerning the baby's disappearance, you will have no difficulty

---

[3] *R v Craig and Bentley*, 9 December 1952.

determining that she is dead, and that she died on the night she disappeared. As to the manner and the cause of death, one cannot be precise because the body was never found. However, what will be proved, largely upon scientific evidence of the baby's clothes, is that the child lost a great deal of blood, in all probability from injury to the major vessels of her neck. She died very quickly because somebody had cut her throat.[4]

[11055] Sometimes a complicated case needs a long opening. If it does, finish with a précis. An example is the criminal case against John Stonehouse, the English MP who faked his drowning in Miami and fled to Australia using a false name. Mr Stonehouse had said he suffered a nervous breakdown. The charges were based on complex financial dealings.[5] Michael Corkery's opening address was very long. He ended in the following way:

Members of the jury, in this case there is no sudden breakdown. This is a story of a crime where a very able and talented man over a period of at least four months covers up his disappearance and spins a web of deception in which almost every single strand is fashioned with ingenuity and great ability. Obviously when caught on Christmas eve there was a great deal of sorrow and torment. You will decide this case on the evidence you will hear. Apply your common sense to the evidence and if you do your honest best no one can complain.[6]

Closing address
The essence of advocacy

[11060] The Supreme Court of Canada approved the following views of a final address:

A closing address is an exercise in advocacy. It is the culmination of a hard fought adversarial proceeding. Crown counsel, like any other advocate is entitled to advance his or her position forcefully and effectively. Juries expect that both counsel will present their positions in that manner and no doubt expect and accept a degree of rhetorical passion in that presentation.[7]

---

[4] John Bryson, *Evil Angels*, 1985, Viking Penguin Books, Ringwood, and Summit Books, New York, p. 347.

[5] *DPP v Stonehouse* [1978] AC 55.

[6] John Stonehouse, *My Trial*, 1976, Wyndham Publications Ltd, London, p. 99.

[7] *R v Rose* [1998] 3 SCR 262; 166 DLR (4th) 385; 129 CCC (3d) 449 at 281; 400; 463 [22].

[11065] The court was right. The final address is advocacy. There are any number of final addresses that are chock-full of emotion, both prosecution and defence. The emotion is more subtle now than it was a century ago. As you read the transcripts of those old trials you will be struck with how florid they were compared with today. Perhaps it is because juries are now more educated. The final address is analytical, acute and skilful, yet still with a thread of passion.

[11070] Its duration will vary depending on the length and complexity of the case. A prosecutor's rule of thumb used to be that the final address should not last more than an hour in an ordinary case. Often the defence final address will last longer. As you read the final addresses of the great American advocate Clarence Darrow you are struck with how long he spoke: six hours here, eight hours there, two days somewhere else! I once addressed a jury for a day in one complex murder trial,[8] and only an hour shorter in another.[9] That's about as long as you would want.

[11075] Above all, don't read your final address. No doubt you have notes. Perhaps you will glance at them occasionally for the page number of the transcript, in order to find a piece of evidence you want to refer to verbatim. The art of advocacy is persuasion. Reading notes is not persuasive. How then do you address without notes? The same way as you question a witness. You will have perhaps a piece of paper with headings and references. Don't be afraid. You will have worked through the final address every night of the trial. Before you stand for the last time you will have worked out the order of your topics. For a failsafe method have all those notes within reach. You won't need them other than for the occasional reference.

Prosecution closing
The striking start

[11080] It is sometimes apt to make a striking start to your closing address. This example is from a rape trial where consent was the central issue:

> Ladies and gentlemen of the jury, you remember what (Ms X) told you she did when at last she got home. Let me remind you of what

---

[8] *R v Gardner*, February 1989 (Victorian Supreme Court).
[9] *R v Churchill*, August 1999 (Western Australian Supreme Court).

she said: "I went upstairs, I was inside the house." Question: "How were you feeling at that time?" Answer: "I couldn't stop crying. Felt hollow. Felt tainted, I guess. It was just unbelievable empty feeling, so I had a shower – I couldn't – I couldn't get the smell off me – this vile stench. I scrubbed myself. I couldn't get rid of it."[10]

Disparaging the defence case

[11085] Ian Barker QC's opening address in the *Chamberlain* case was referred to above.[11] In his final address he examined all the evidence about the dingo taking the baby. He went through it item by item and submitted that there was no evidence of the presence of a dingo. This is how he finished this part of his final address:

> Supposing the dingo was on trial here. How would you possibly convict it on this evidence? Where is the evidence? Where is there one substantial clue, apart from the account given by the child's mother, pointing to a killing of this child by a dingo? There isn't one. The case against the dingo would be laughed out of court.[12]

Defence closing
Planning

[11090] The defence closing address will have been planned before the trial started. Cross-examination will have been directed to obtaining evidence solely for use in the closing address. It is the advocate's chance to draw together all of the threads in the evidence to weave into a coherent fabric. For the reason that every case has its own special qualities, I will simply give some examples.

Knowledge of human affairs

[11095] Ronald Griggs was charged with the murder of his wife. He was a Methodist minister. At the time of her death he was having an affair with another woman. In 1928 this was adultery and considered

---

10   This example is quoted by Justice Trevor Riley in his book *The Little Red Book of Advocacy*, 2003, Law Society of the Northern Territory, p. 78. The case was *R v Knight & Ors*, February 2000 before Riley J and jury.

11   See [11050].

12   John Bryson, *Evil Angels* op cit p. 515.

not just wrong but immoral and a serious sin. It was made even worse because of the accused's position. The prosecution case was that the affair was the motive for the murder. Listen to how George Maxwell KC dealt with this aspect, showing his own knowledge of how people function, and how he told the jury about it.[13] He acknowledged the wrongdoing but denied the motive.

> Considerable reference has been made to the accused being a Methodist minister. He was a minister of the Gospel, and he has been held up to opprobrium because of his acts with this woman Condon. One cannot say a single word in extenuation of his conduct regarding his marital affairs, of his double life while carrying on his duties as a minister of religion. But, when a man dons clerical garb, gentlemen, it doesn't mean that he becomes less human and liable to human temptations than any other man. It is a repetition of a story as old as creation. Another instance of the subtle attractions of woman for man and man for woman.
>
> Estrangement had begun between himself and his wife, for other reasons . . . They had not known each other very much before marriage, and they had found out afterwards that they were not much suited to each other.[14]

Expert evidence

[11100] Most criminal cases have some form of expert evidence. Some of it the defence contests. Your address to the jury on this subject will be based on the evidence, the contradictions, the absence of the right tests, the failure to take all relevant matters into account, and so on. The final address on this topic will probably begin with the proposition that this is trial by jury, not trial by expert. In the *Chamberlain* case, Muirhead J directed the jury immaculately. His sentiments and common sense are worthy of a final address. Leaving out the formal politenesses, his Honour said:

> There is no magic about the opinions of experts because they, like any of us, can make errors: not only because they may work on theories that others may not share, but also because an opinion can only be as good and valid as the facts on which it is based. So factual error:

---

[13] "Maxwell was the greatest criminal advocate I ever heard." "His power was in the address to the jury, which was quite hypnotic.": Sir Robert Menzies, *The Measure of the Years*, 1970, Cassell, Australia, pp. 254, 255.

[14] A J Buchanan, *The Trial of Ronald Geeves Griggs*, 1930, Law Book Co, Sydney, pp. 194–195.

error in theory: error in methodology may invalidate an opinion, however persuasively based . . .[15]

[11105] Here is Maxwell KC, again in *R v Griggs*. Mrs Griggs had died by poisoning from arsenic. How it was administered and whether by one or two doses were important issues. She could have taken it accidentally. She might have committed suicide when she found out about the affair her husband was having. Maxwell KC had cross-examined the pathologist, Dr Mollison, at length.[16] Here is his final address on Dr Mollison:

> But what does the evidence say? Dr Mollison gives it as his opinion that there were different doses, but under cross-examination, he made several admissions on this point which made his opinion worthless. He admitted that, if one dose only had been taken, it might be possible for a part to flow away and remain in the large intestine, while the remainder was retained in the stomach, not absorbed.
>
> According to the Crown, Mrs Griggs was given a large dose of arsenic, which Dr Mollison admits could only be administered in a cupful of liquid, at a time when Mrs Mitchell says the dead woman was only capable of taking sips.
>
> The Crown case is that this monster of iniquity in the dock, to make absolutely sure of killing his wife, somehow forced down her throat a cupful of liquid containing an enormous dose of arsenic.
>
> Applying commonsense to it, Dr Mollison's evidence is reduced to nonsense. It seems to me that these scientists are led away by theory. There is no question as to Dr Mollison's fairness, but if you apply ordinary commonsense arguments, you will come to the conclusion that there is not a tittle of the evidence before you inconsistent with the idea that only one dose was taken by Mrs Griggs.[17]

The homely example

[11110] Advocates are in constant search of the homely example to illustrate a point. Here is one example to illustrate that the prosecution must prove its case. It was a murder case. The defence was that the accused did not kill, and the culprit must have been someone else. During the case the defence pointed to others who had serious

---

[15] J H Muirhead, *A Brief Summing Up*, 1996, Access Press, Northbridge WA, pp. 163–164.
[16] For the start of the cross-examination see Chapter 7 [7025].
[17] A J Buchanan, op cit, pp 203–204.

anger towards the victim, whereas the accused and the victim had always got on well.

The prosecution must prove its case and prove it beyond reasonable doubt. There is no other fair way of doing it. Because the Crown chooses its ground, because the Crown has the running of the case, they bring the charge, let them prove it. What would be the situation if the onus were on us, as the prosecutor has suggested, and wrongly suggested to you, that it's up to us to show that there's another person who is likely to have committed the crime?

Can you imagine me in this position. Let's say that someone rings Woolworths at 5 o'clock last night and tells them that there is a bomb planted in their Knuckey Street store. Someone traces the call and they say it came from a public phone booth from over the road. The police come round to me and say, "What were you doing yesterday at 5 pm?"

I say, "Well, I finished in court and I took my robes off and I walked down the street."

They say, "Anywhere near Knuckey Street?"

"Yes."

"Did you make that phone call?"

I say, "No."

They say, "Was anyone with you at the time?"

I say, "No."

They say, "We're going to charge you with this. You can come along to court and prove that you were not the person who made the phone call."

I say, "Hold on a minute, I had Mr Bauman with me. We were both walking down Knuckey Street."

They say, "Even better. We'll charge the both of you and you can decide between you who's the guilty one and who's the not guilty one."[18]

Summary

[11115] To prepare a prosecution opening address to a jury:

1. Use ordinary English.
2. Start with a short outline of the whole case.
3. Do not refer to evidence in dispute. Never refer to an accused giving evidence.

[18] *R v Tipungwuti* (Northern Territory Supreme Court) 9 August 1989. The accused was acquitted.

4. Describe the offence but never refer to the penalty.
5. Speak simply of the presumption of innocence and the onus of proof.
6. Mention proof beyond reasonable doubt but never define it.
7. Give more detail of the evidence. Identify the main witnesses. If appropriate, introduce photographs, plans or charts. Do not refer to a defence unless it is obvious.
8. Use a good order, especially logical order. Perhaps a chronology is useful.
9. Describe the functions of judge, jury, prosecutor and defence counsel.
10. Open conservatively lest the evidence fails to support you. Avoid emotion.

[11120] To prepare a closing address before a jury:

1. Isolate the issues from your preparation, from the evidence, and if in doubt by confirming them with the judge.
2. Prepare and use a logical order.
3. Use ordinary English.
4. Speak directly to the jury in a natural voice using your own style. Use timing and volume and a little emotion where necessary. Don't read from notes. Try to appear sincere.
5. Answer your opponent's strong points. Do not descend to trifles. Never belittle your opponent personally.
6. In a criminal case do not even allude to the penalty.
7. Never give your own opinion or refer to matters not in evidence.
8. If you refer to law make sure it is correct. Never undermine a judge's ruling.
9. In a criminal case refer to the presumption of innocence and the onus of proof. Never define "beyond reasonable doubt". In a civil case you can define "balance of probabilities".
10. Draw commonsense conclusions from the evidence. Use homely examples.

Chapter 12

Plea in mitigation

Introduction

[12000] Most people charged with a criminal offence plead guilty. The task of the defence advocate is to persuade the sentencer to impose the lowest possible punishment. The art is to allow the sentencer to become convinced that the most appropriate disposition happens to be the most lenient one.

[12005] The plea in mitigation is a harrowing procedure for the person who has pleaded guilty or been found guilty. The offender, whose immediate future depends on the outcome, is probably feeling both repentant and fearful about the result. It is a hugely responsible task for the sentencer who needs to tailor a sentence to fit the crime and the offender. The duty of the advocate is correspondingly important. It calls for a good deal more than the recitation of some well-worn formula or string of stale phrases.

> Sentencing judges must be vigilant to ensure that they do not accept uncritically at face value all submissions to the effect that the person standing for sentence is "at the crossroads", "has seen the error of his ways", "is at a turning point of his life", or "has excellent prospects of rehabilitation". Often such submissions have no justification in fact and are based on no more than wishful thinking.[1]

[12010] In this part I will not deal with the person who has been found guilty after trial by jury. The jury might have returned its verdict rejecting defence evidence of good character, which was led to show the unlikelihood of the person's guilt. The plea in mitigation is often quite short because the sentencer has heard a good deal of what would otherwise be plea material as part of the trial.

---

[1] *R v Govinden* (1999) 106 A Crim R 314 (NSW CCA) per Dunford J at 319 [35].

[12015] The word "plea" has two meanings. The first is when a person is charged with a criminal offence and asked "How do you plead: guilty or not guilty." That is the arraignment. The other meaning of "plea" is the evidence and submissions in mitigation of penalty.

Preparation

[12020] Preparation is as important for a plea as for any appearance in court. The task of the prosecuting advocate is largely over when the accused pleads guilty. But the defence advocate has a great deal of work to do. So these thoughts are now directed to the defence. You will need full instructions from your client. You will need instructions from the witnesses to the events over which the charges were laid. All the while you will need to look at the law and at the prosecution evidence to decide whether any charges can be made good by the prosecution.

[12025] Almost every chapter in this book emphasises the need for careful preparation. Consider how Muirhead J characterised the plea in *Putti v Simpson*:

> I hope this court will seldom have to entertain an appeal such as this where the basic ground for allowing the appeal is that the defendant's counsel in the court below was not only unprepared for the task, but permitted matters to proceed without taking effective steps to ensure his client's case was eventually put carefully and clearly to the court.[2]

Lack of proper preparation not only undermines the case for your client, it also shows grave disrespect for the court and for justice.

[12030] If you are satisfied that your analysis shows that the better course is to plead guilty, then the preparation begins with that in mind. When the hearing of the plea begins, you will want to give the sentencer a list of the things you are intending to do and on which your submission will be based. Start preparing. Which witnesses would help the submission? A psychologist? The employer? Against all odds can you call your client? Find the sentencing principles and the tariff, which is the minimum period prescribed by statute. What is the maximum and the going rate imposed by courts for similar offences and offenders? Does your client show remorse, have any prior convictions or accept the need for reparation?

---

[2] *Putti v Simpson* (1975) 6 ALR 47 at 51 (NT, Muirhead J).

The decision on how to plead

[12035] The decision on how to plead is the first to make. People have pleaded guilty to a charge of murder when the sentence was death.[3] The decision whether to plead guilty or not guilty will include:

1. Instructions from the accused.
2. The nature of the charge.
3. The likelihood of the accused's being found guilty.
4. The advantage in penalty by pleading guilty.

[12040] Sometimes you have no choice. You make an offer to the prosecution and it is rejected. The trial begins because there is no alternative. During the trial the prosecution may make the offer to you. It does not happen very often at all. But it did occur in *R v Parker and Mulhall*.[4] The two accused pleaded not guilty to murder. The prosecution opened its case and the defence responded. The first witnesses were called and cross-examined. Then the prosecution came to the defence and offered manslaughter. The defence accepted. The plea for both accused took a day.

[12045] You should go to trial where you form the conclusion that the prosecution cannot prove some element of its case or when you have a good defence. Only once have I refused to accept instructions from an accused to plead guilty. His reasons for wanting to plead guilty were that he just wanted the rape charge to be finished even though the woman had consented. We went to trial and he was acquitted.

Negotiating the lowest charge

[12050] A decision to plead guilty will sometimes depend on whether the prosecution will accept a plea to the offence that you think is appropriate. The negotiation can begin in any number of ways. In the superior courts the defence will often send a written submission to the Director of Public Prosecutions suggesting that a lesser charge is the correct one. A common submission is that manslaughter is the proper charge rather than murder. There are occasions when the offer in writing has come from the prosecution.[5]

---

[3] *R v Vent* (1935) 25 Cr App R 55; *R v Bliss* [1937] 1 DLR 1; *R v Pearce* [1953] Tas LR 69; *R v David* [1966] VR 358. Sentence of death was pronounced in each case.

[4] *R v Parker and Mulhall* (2002) 131 A Crim R 597.

[5] For example, *R v Kolalich* (1990) 47 A Crim R 71.

Sometimes it is quite informal, such as by telephone call between defence and prosecution. The important duty borne by the prosecuting advocate in the public interest is to accept a plea to the correct offence and nothing less.

[12055] In the lowest courts the settlement of the appropriate charge will usually be informal and often occur as late as the day on which the charge is listed for mention or hearing.

Settling the facts

[12060] In some places the prosecution and defence agree on the facts, which are put in writing. The procedure is that after the accused is arraigned and pleads guilty, the prosecutor reads the facts to the court. The judge asks the defence whether those facts are agreed. Almost invariably the judge will sentence on those facts.

[12065] The agreed facts should include every matter of substance. This will show the relevance of the decision to plead guilty. It will also prevent a person being charged again over episodes that are included. When the facts are agreed they should be read out for the purpose of the transcript.[6]

[12070] Occasionally the facts are not settled. Where the charge is right but the facts are in dispute the judge must hear evidence. The rule is that mitigating facts are to be proved on balance of probabilities and aggravating facts must be proved beyond reasonable doubt.[7] There may be some questions of fact that a judge will find difficult or impossible to solve and which may not cause an increase or decrease in the sentence.[8]

Other convictions and antecedents

[12075] Convictions that are entered before the commission of the present offence often have a real bearing on sentence. A second conviction for the same offence will often attract a minimum penalty by law. Driving offences are an obvious example. But the general risk to an accused of earlier convictions is that the sentencer will say that the prospects of rehabilitation are small: the earlier conviction taught nothing.

---

[6] *GAS v The Queen* (2004) 217 CLR 198 at 214–215 [42]–[44].

[7] *R v Olbrich* (1999) 199 CLR 270.

[8] *Weininger v The Queen* (2003) 212 CLR 629.

[12080] Convictions later than the offence for which the accused is being sentenced can also have an effect. What would otherwise be mitigating is given less weight. A sentencer is entitled to say that the present offence is not an aberration.

[12085] In short, a sentencer can take into account the accused's antecedents.[9] Those antecedents may determine whether the proper disposition is at one extreme a diversion program or a sentence of imprisonment at the other extreme. The sentencer must make sure that the sentence is proper for the offence. It is wrong to sentence for other conduct. It is also wrong to sentence a wrongdoer to imprisonment for his or her own good, such as to dry out[10] or to be given some formal education.[11]

Psychiatric difficulties or impaired intelligence

[12090] If you suspect from the papers you read and from the instructions you receive that the accused has psychiatric difficulties or impaired intelligence, then you must have an assessment made. You should get an expert opinion from a psychiatrist or a psychologist.

[12095] When an accused person has such a difficulty, the sentencer must note that it has the following effect on sentence:

1. It may reduce the moral culpability for the offence.
2. It may have a bearing on the type of sentence.
3. General deterrence is moderated.
4. Specific deterrence is often not worth pursuing.
5. A sentence will weigh more heavily on such a person than on one in normal health.[12]

Effect on the victim

[12100] A sentencer will take special notice of the effect that the offence has had on a victim. There is some tension in the law on the

---

[9] *Veen v The Queen* [No 2] (1988) 164 CLR 465 at 477–478.

[10] *Ngulkurr v O'Brien* (1989) 98 FLR 279; 45 A Crim R 92 (Kearney J).

[11] *Nelson v Chute* (1994) 72 A Crim R 85 at 90 (Martin CJ).

[12] *R v Champion* (1992) 64 A Crim R 244 at 254–255; *R v Tsiaras* [1996] 1 VR 398 at 400; *R v Yaldiz* [1998] 2 VR 396 at 381; *R v Bux* (2002) 132 A Crim R 395 at 403 [34]; *R v Bridger* [2003] 1 NZLR 636; *Thompson v The Queen* (2005) 157 A Crim R 385 at 395–396 [52]–[55].

subject, for in a homicide case the sentence is not to be greater for the death of a loved victim than for an unloved victim.[13]

[12105] The prosecuting advocate will often serve a victim impact statement on the defence with a view to filing it in the court before the plea starts. This statement shows the special effects of the offence on the victim and on those close to the victim. The statement should not contain inadmissible material.[14]

Parity and totality

[12110] The sentencer should make the sentence of each accused as equal as possible. What will cause a variation in the sentences will mainly be the different parts played, and the differences in age, antecedents and general character.[15] Where a single accused pleads guilty to more than one offence, the sentencer will impose a proper sentence on each offence, then make concurrency orders so that the total sentence is not overwhelming.[16]

Age

[12115] Age makes a difference to sentence. A juvenile will tend to be treated with some lenience, for the offence might be seen as a youthful aberration. An elderly person will likewise get some leniency. Gaol for such a person could eat up most of the remaining years.

[12120] A person who has reached middle years without conviction may call evidence of good character maintained for so long. The principle applies to property offences[17] as well as to offences of violence.[18]

The last run-through before the plea

[12125] Make sure you have left nothing out in your preparation. Check the statements and depositions of each witness. Analyse and

---

[13] *R v Previtera* (1997) 94 A Crim R 76 at 86–87; *Mitchell v The Queen* (1998) 20 WAR 201; 104 A Crim R 523.

[14] *R v Dowlan* [1998] 1 VR 123 at 140 per Charles JA; *Mitchell v The Queen* (1998) 20 WAR 257 at 268 per Ipp J.

[15] *Lowe v The Queen* (1984) 154 CLR 606 at 609. See also *R v Talia* [1996] 1 VR 462 at 484 ff.

[16] *Pearce v The Queen* (1998) 194 CLR 610 at 624 [45]; *DPP v Grabovac* [1998] 1 VR 664 at 680.

[17] *R v Smith* (1982) 7 A Crim R 437 at 442 per Starke J.

[18] *R v Okutgen* (1982) 8 A Crim R 262 at 265–266.

note the record of interview. There are times when you can make some assertions of fact from the Bar table, but the judgment as to when to make them and on what is usually a function of experience. One wise judge said:

> [I]t has long been the practice in the criminal jurisdiction to accept and act on factual statements (particularly as to the personal background of an offender) advanced from the bar table, unless they are disputed as to their accuracy or otherwise questioned by the prosecution, or, in the circumstances of the case, there is some positive, apparent reason to doubt their accuracy.
>
> Were it otherwise, the business of the Courts would grind to a halt.[19]

It is better to err on the side of caution and give the prosecution notice of what you suspect may be disputed matters.

[12130] Do the circumstances need to be debated or explained, or are there aspects about the unfolding of the event that do your client credit? Can you point the sentencer to evidence of remorse and prospects of rehabilitation? Does the accused have good character, or are there convictions and unhelpful antecedents that must be explained? Do you have the law on the principles that apply and on the generally accepted penalty for this offence? Are there witnesses to call from whom you have instructions? Will you take the ultimate chance of calling the accused to give evidence?

[12135] Next arrange the topics in the sequence you think best. Write down the heading of each topic so you can give the sentencer an outline to start with. That has the added advantage of ordering your thoughts. Now you are ready.

The plea

[12140] After the accused has been arraigned and pleaded guilty, the plea will begin. Start the plea slowly with an outline of the course the plea is going to take. These are your headings. You may even take the last step here and tell the sentencer what you will submit is the appropriate sentence. You will have to judge the wisdom of this course. Here is an example, but it is only an example. Your plea will be different because it will be one-off, tailor made, custom built.

---

[19] *Gumurdul v Reinke* (2006) 161 A Crim R 87 at 94–95 [48]–[49] (Olsson AJ). But remember the warning of Muirhead J set out above in [12025].

I propose to address you on the following matters:

1. The circumstances of the offence.
2. Matters personal to the prisoner.
3. Answers in the police interview showing remorse.
4. I will call evidence of good character from the prisoner's employer.
5. I will call evidence of community good works from the Red Cross.
6. This evidence is designed to show good prospects of rehabilitation.

I will then move to the case law to show:

1. The mitigating effects of a plea of guilty.
2. Principles of sentencing a person of this age and background.
3. The tariff for this offence.

I will last of all submit what is the appropriate disposition.

You will then develop each point.

[12145] This advance summary is wonderful for the sentencer, who will know at any time the purpose of any submission you make. The sentencer will probably say, "You need not address me on the mitigating effects of a plea of guilty. I know and accept the law on that." What a help!

[12150] My final suggestion is that you start low-key on fairly uncontentious matters, and build as the plea goes on.

Appeal

[12155] There is no appeal other than by statute. Legislation now gives the prosecution and the defence the right to appeal against a sentence. The usual basis is that the sentence is plainly wrong. The prosecution says it is manifestly inadequate or the defence says it is manifestly excessive. Because the wrongness of the sentence is claimed to be manifest, no sustained argument is necessary or even allowed. The excess or inadequacy is manifest or it is not.

[12160] Other defence grounds of appeal usually allege that the sentencing judge made some error that can be identified. It might have been an error of fact, such as attributing a prominence to the offence not borne out of the evidence. It might have been an error of law such as saying that the maximum penalty is greater than it is, or dismissing the effect of a plea of guilty.[20] I deal with these matters in the next chapter.

---

[20] See Chapter 13 Appeals.

Chapter 13

Appeals

General

[13000] An appeal is a call to a higher tribunal to alter the decision of a lower one.

[13005] The best-known type of appeal is from the decision of a jury in a criminal case. Counsel for a convicted person will tell an appeal court that the judge allowed wrong evidence to be given or stopped evidence being given that should have been allowed. An excellent example is where a court set aside a conviction because a trial judge had wrongly used discretion to allow a jury to hear evidence of a confession made under duress in a foreign country.[1]

[13010] There may be an argument that the judge did not give proper directions to the jury. An example is *Green*, where the accused said that his confession was false. The appeal against conviction was allowed because the trial judge did not tell the jury that there is no presumption that a confession is true.[2]

[13015] On sentence an accused can argue that the sentencer was in error or that the sentence was manifestly excessive. By more recent statute, the prosecution can now appeal on error or because there is manifest inadequacy in the sentence.

[13020] But an appeal can take many forms, usually depending on where the case was first heard. The decision of a minister can go to the Administrative Appeals Tribunal. In fact there can be an appeal from all sort of administrative decisions.[3]

---

[1] *R v Thomas* (2006) 163 A Crim R 567 (Vic CA).
[2] *R v Green* (2002) 4 VR 471 especially at 481 [31] (CA).
[3] Preston J, "Judicial Review of illegality and irrationality of administrative decisions in Australia" (2006) 28 Aust Bar Rev 17–40.

[13025] These appeals are just over a century old. Before then there was no law allowing an appeal. The power for a court to hear appeals usually comes from the legislation that sets up a new superior court.[4]

Creature of statute

[13030] An appeal is not a remedy of the common law. The power to appeal comes only from statute. Kirby J put it this way:

> Appeal is not a creature of the common law. It is invariably the creature of statute. To assess, where challenged, the purported exercise of a party of a right to appeal . . . it is essential to scrutinise the suggested legislative foundation for such a right and jurisdiction. If it cannot be demonstrated in the language, or in the implications to be derived from the language, of the relevant statute, the right and jurisdiction asserted do not exist. The common law cannot be invoked to fill silences in the legislation.[5]

[13035] There are four main forms of appeal from the statutes:

1. A true appeal, where the judgment before the trial court was correct on the material before it.
2. An appeal by way of rehearing on the evidence before the trial court.
3. An appeal by way of rehearing supplemented by other evidence.
4. An appeal by way of hearing anew.[6]

[13040] There is one other form of getting a higher court to consider whether the lower court was right in law. That is a case stated. (See below [1360–1380].)

Preparation

[13045] An appeal takes a great deal of preparation. In many jurisdictions, the practice is for the trial advocate not to do the appeal. There are a number of reasons for that. First, a new mind is brought into the case. Second, the trial advocate might have made some tactical decisions that could be hard to explain, or at worst may be professionally embarrassing. Third, in the high-level appeal courts, the drafting of the court papers and the conduct of the appeal is

---

[4] *Sweeney v Fitzhardinge* (1906) 4 CLR 716 per Griffith CJ at 725.

[5] *Byrnes v The Queen* (1999) 199 CLR 1 at 35 [84].

[6] *Fox v Percy* (2003) 214 CLR 118 at 124–125 [20] per Gleeson CJ, Gummow and Kirby JJ after considering earlier decisions.

sometimes regarded as a specialty within itself. Some advocates are champions at trial but not on appeal.

[13050] If you are brought into an appeal in a case you haven't dealt with before, there is one thing you must do. Make sure you have all of the papers, including the transcript of the evidence and any exhibits. Then you must immerse yourself in the facts of the case and the law that may apply. There is no shortcut. But if there be a principle of preparation it is this. Get a full knowledge of the evidence. Decide what the facts should be. Then stand above the whole case to find out in law whether the decision below was right or wrong. Once you have read and analysed all of the papers you will have to decide three things. Did the court below make a mistake? How? With what result?

[13055] If you conclude that the court below made a serious mistake of law alone, then you will consider whether the proper method of getting the case before a higher court is by case stated.

Case stated

[13060] As for all methods of getting a case to a higher court, the entitlement is set out in legislation. Of course the legislation will vary between jurisdictions but its essence is the same throughout. The papers in the case must show that on the facts that the lower court found, there was an error of law.

[13065] The case stated procedure is fairly refined and only of special use where law alone is involved. It cannot be a complaint about the wrong use of discretion. The facts must be the facts found by the lower court. The lower court must have the power to state a case. Some tribunals do not have that power.[7] Even a court that can ordinarily state a case may lose it because of the nature of the hearing. An example of the loss of that power is a Magistrates' Court hearing a committal.[8] If the case stated is not based on fact but on argument,[9] or if the facts are not relevant,[10] the higher court will not entertain it. As one judge said, a case stated is not a judicial roving commission.[11]

---

[7] For example, *Frost v AMACA* (2004) 61 NSWLR 158 (CA).

[8] *Ebatarinja v Price* (1997) 137 FLR 281 (NT, Mildren J).

[9] *Wallin v Curtain* (1998) 100 A Crim R 506 (Vic CA).

[10] *Furze v Nixon* (2000) 2 VR 503 (CA).

[11] *Attorney-General's Reference (No 3 of 1994)* [1998] AC 245 at 265 per Lord Mustill.

[13070] The procedure is a demanding one on the advocate. You must draft the relevant facts found by the court. Then you draft the questions of law. You submit them to the lower court judicial officer, who you hope will sign them. This completes the documentation, which then goes to the higher court. You must not attach a transcript of the evidence.[12] In a rare case the judge may refuse to state a case and the higher court will direct that it be done.[13]

[13075] When a case stated is appropriate, it produces exactly what the advocate wants – a decision on a point of law. One example will do. Is a male transsexual, who has sex-changing surgery and dresses to pass as a female, a female or a male? That was the essence of the question posed and answered in *Harris*.[14] Otherwise it is a cumbersome,[15] limited and unsatisfactory procedure.[16] More stylish and allowing reference to a great deal of material are applications for prerogative writs or a straight out appeal. But when the case stated does work, it works like a dream.[17]

[13080] The tests you will use to decide whether you should proceed by case stated will be these:

1. Has a lower court decided facts?
2. Do those facts involve a question of law?
3. Was the question of law raised in the lower court?
4. Does the lower court have the power to state a case?
5. Is stating a case the best procedure?

Analysis

[13085] The first thing you must do is to look at the legislation that allows an appeal. You cannot get an appeal court to decide the case without its having the power to do so. If you do appeal in these circumstances, a court will declare that it does not have jurisdiction.

---

[12] *R v Madden* (1999) 85 A Crim R 385 (NSW CCA) at 370–371 per Hunt CJ.

[13] An example is the decision of the Full Court in *Freeman v Harris* [1980] VR 267 at 268.

[14] *R v Harris* (1988) 17 NSWLR 158; 35 A Crim R 146 (CCA).

[15] *Collins v State Rail Authority of New South Wales* (1986) 5 NSWLR 209 (CA) at 211 per Street CJ.

[16] *R v Rowe* (2004) 50 NSWLR 510 (CCA) at 513 [9] per Fitzgerald JA.

[17] Examples are *Re Anne Hamilton-Byrne* [1995] 1 VR 129 (FC); *Director of Public Prosecutions (No 1 of 1999)* (1999) 8 NTLR 148 (Martin CJ); *R v Crehan and Rowe* (2001) 4 VR 189 (CA).

An example is *R (McCann) v Manchester Crown Court* where the House of Lords did just that: declare that it had no power.[18]

[13090] Start working out what went wrong with the case at the lower court. If you do find an error, check to see whether that point was taken below. If the point you find has not been taken in the court below, there will be great difficulty in persuading an appeal court to uphold it. This principle applies in a criminal case.[19] Of course the ultimate test is whether there has been a miscarriage of justice or an unfair trial. But as Walters J said, a point not taken at trial should not lightly be made a ground of appeal.[20]

[13095] The principle about appealing on a point not taken below is applied with even more force in a civil case. The High Court heard a personal injury case where the main point had not been argued at the trial. In a joint judgment three of the justices said this:

> It would be inimical to the due administration of justice if, on appeal, a party could raise a point that was not taken at trial. Nothing is more likely to give rise to a sense of injustice in a litigant than to have a verdict taken away on a point that was not taken at trial and could or might possibly have been met by rebutting evidence or cross-examination.[21]

[13100] A complaint about procedure will fall on deaf ears on appeal if there had been nothing said earlier. In one case Judge George Meerabux was dismissed from office because of misbehaviour.[22] The hearing was in camera. The judge was represented by counsel and did not complain about the procedure. The Privy Council advised that a complaint to it about the hearing in camera had no basis.[23]

Drafting

[13105] There are some do's and don'ts about drafting the grounds. The main thing is to draft a ground that you think will win. Don't descend to trifling grounds. Draft them as if you are going to argue

---

[18] *R (McCann) v Manchester Crown Court* [2003] 1 AC 787.

[19] *Stirland v DPP* [1944] AC 319 at 328; *R v Donald* (1983) 34 SASR 10 at 25. See also Chapter 10 [10110].

[20] *R v Lavery* (1979) 20 SASR 430 at 431 per Walters J.

[21] *Whisprun Pty Ltd v Dixon* (2003) 77 ALJR 1598 at 1608 [51] per Gleeson CJ, McHugh and Gummow JJ. Applied *Financial Wisdom Ltd v Newman* (2005) 12 VR 79 at 113 [84] (CA).

[22] *Meerabux v Attorney-General of Belize* [2005] 2 AC 513 at at 522 [9] sets out the complaints.

[23] *Meerabux v Attorney-General of Belize* at 533 [41].

them, and as you draft keep the argument in mind.[24] The evidence and the judge's decisions on the law will be the basis of most grounds. So the grounds and the law in support work in tandem. You must set out the grounds you expect to win. If you leave out a ground and think of it only when arguing, the court will rarely allow you to add that ground.[25]

[13110] Courts have described trifling grounds in a rather disparaging way. Some courts refer to armchair appeals:

> ... an 'armchair appeal' where, after the trial, counsel not involved in the trial has sat down and gone through the whole of the transcript and summing up looking for error without reference to the manner in which the trial was conducted.[26]

In one unfortunate case a Full Court described a ground as pettifoggery.[27]

Facts already found

[13115] Once you have drafted the grounds it is then a matter of writing the submissions. You must realise, when you are drafting the submissions and arguing the appeal, that a decision by the lower court has already been made. As one eminent silk wrote, the slate is not clean.[28] You must make the hard decision of what to attack and what to concede. Soon enough your opponent will draft a response. Read it carefully. It too will make concessions and put matters in issue. How will this affect your arguments? Once you have done the hard analysis, try to nut out the questions that the judges are likely to ask and what your answers will be.

[13120] Don't overlook the fact that the court below has seen and heard the witnesses and come to a conclusion on whom to believe. The judge might not have referred to demeanour. As McHugh J said:

> When a trial judge resolves a conflict of evidence between witnesses, the subtle influence of demeanour cannot be overlooked . . . In

---

[24] In *R v B* [1966] 1 WLR 1612; [1966] 3 All ER 496 Lord Parker CJ said that counsel should only draft grounds (at 1613; 496) "which they feel they are in a position to come before the court and seek to uphold."

[25] *R v Haycraft* (1974) 54 Cr App R 121 (CCA).

[26] *R v Mahoney* (2000) 114 A Crim R 130 at 134 [15] (NSW CCA). This metaphor has been used again and again. See *R v Fuge* (2001) 123 A Crim R 310 at 319 [40] and *R v Fowler* (2003) 151 A Crim R 166 at 175 [38].

[27] *Woods v Rogers; Ex parte Woods* [1983] 2 Qd R 212 at 215.

[28] DF Jackson QC, "Appellate advocacy" (1992) 8 Aust Bar Rev 245–254.

accordance with the rules relating to the review of findings of fact based in whole or in part on demeanour, those findings are not open to review in an appellate court.[29]

[13125] So be cautious indeed about arguing on appeal that the court below could not have properly come to certain findings of fact when there was supporting evidence.

Fresh evidence

[13130] An exception to the rule excluding an appeal on a point not taken in the court below is where there is important fresh evidence. The evidence must have arisen since the lower court's decision. Evidence that was available but not led at trial is not fresh. Needless to say, the court must have the power to hear fresh evidence. Some courts have said that they do not have that jurisdiction.[30] But when the court does have the power it will entertain the submission in a civil case.[31] In a criminal case the appeal court will apply tests to decide whether it will accept the fresh evidence.[32]

[13135] One court has said that the following procedure must be adopted. You must give notice of the application to adduce fresh evidence. The proposed fresh evidence must be presented in an affidavit. The other parties must be served and the documents filed in court.[33]

Practice

[13140] Many appeal courts have strict rules that they use to refine procedure. Those rules govern what and when documents must be filed, and what they must contain. To find out what those rules are first, look on the internet. If that fails, the Registrar of the court will point you in the right direction. Most of them are extremely obliging. Speak to a practitioner whose practice is mostly in the appeal court about the best pre-appeal procedures. The practitioner

---

[29] *Jones v Hyde* (1989) ALJR 349 at 351; 85 ALR 23 at 27–28 per McHugh J with whom all the other Justices agreed. His Honour repeated the first of these propositions in *Abalos v Australian Postal Commission* (1990) 171 CLR at 179.

[30] The High Court says it has no power to hear fresh evidence: *Mickelberg v The Queen* (1989) 167 CLR 259; *Eastman v The Queen* (2000) 203 CLR 1.

[31] For example, *Cowan v Council of the City of Greater Wollongong* (1954) 54 SR (NSW) 264 and on appeal by the defendant council (1955) 93 CLR 435.

[32] *R v Nguyen* [1998] 4 VR 394 at 400–401 (CA).

[33] *Benedetto v The Queen* [2003] 1 WLR 1545 at 1575 [76] (PC).

will give you all sorts of hints about drafting, about how to address the court and lots more.

[13145] The next thing to find out is whether you have an appeal as of right or whether you have to ask for leave to appeal. If you need leave to appeal there is often a time limit on how long you can speak. So whatever the practice, go along to court. Listen to those counsel who spend a lot of their court time there. Watch the judges. Nearly all of them work very hard in and out of court. Some will be charming, while others will not be able to ask counsel a question without sneering. Work out what you think are the best techniques for presenting your argument.

In court

[13150] The appeal court has all the documents – yours and your opponent's. The experienced advocates will tell you that you can expect some surprises in a court of appeal. Occasionally you will come across a judge who has read no documents and done no homework at all. Another judge may not only have analysed everything, but already written a judgment in draft. The only changes to the draft judgment will come from how the arguments are presented.

[13155] There is an advantage in speaking first. You have a chance to capture the court. Proceed directly to the argument. As Mason CJ said:

> Too often counsel fail to take advantage of the unique opportunity presented by the opening – to make an impact on the minds of the judges before they begin to move forward on their inexorable journey to a conclusion. There is no need for a ritual incantation of the history of the litigation. The Court is aware of it. Better to start with a statement of the issues, unless the case lands itself to an exhilarating or humorous introduction.[34]

[13160] Simply refer to the ground of appeal and then develop the arguments in support.[35] I would not recommend a humorous introduction. I have never used it. Nor do any experienced appellate advocates begin like that. Let the last word on the subject come from one of the most experienced, who said not to start that way:

---

[34] Mason CJ (1984) 58 ALJ 537 "The role of counsel and appellate advocacy" at 542.
[35] So said Heydon J in "Reciprocal duties of Bench and Bar" (2007) 81 ALJ 23 at 32.

Witty observations which blossomed in chambers tend to wilt in the more acid rain of the courtroom.[36]

Watch and listen

[13165] Watch the bench and listen. It goes without saying that you must never interrupt a judge who is speaking. But there are more important reasons for watching and listening. One example will do. You will have worked out an order of your submissions. A judge might ask you a question that interrupts your intended order. Do you say that you will deal with that point later, or do you answer the question you are asked? The answer is simple. Answer the question. Do not be concerned if it throws your plan out of kilter. If you say that you will answer in due course, the judge will lose some interest. Besides, the judges run the court, not you. But do be careful of the answers you give to those questions. Plenty of appeal court judges were classy advocates before they went on the bench. They know how to ask what seems like an innocuous series of questions. Plenty of us have answered those questions, only to find that what we said destroyed our appeal.

[13170] Sometimes two judges may start talking to one another. You expect that it is a point that arises on the appeal. There is no point in continuing to talk. Stop. Wait. When the judges have finished their talk they will perhaps ask you a question or at least tell you to go on.

Precedent

[13175] Precedent is legal principle developed by a higher court, which is binding on a lower one. Precedent avoids uncertainty.[37] There is a hierarchy of courts.[38] There will be times in your written and spoken submissions that you will want to refer to the decision of another court. But there are some important points to remember. An appeal court may not feel so bound by decisions as does a trial court. But whether binding or persuasive, you may want to refer to the decision of another court. Your opponent's submissions may cite cases, which you need to show are not helpful.

---

[36] DF Jackson QC, "Appellate advocacy" (1992) 8 Aust Bar Rev 245 at 250.

[37] *Re Hallett's Estate* (1880) 13 Ch D 696 at 797–798 per Sir George Jessell MR; *D'Orta-Ekenaike v Victoria Legal Aid* (2005) 233 CLR 1 at 79–80 [244]–[245] per Kirby J.

[38] *Cassell & Co v Broome* [1972] AC 1027 at 1054 per Lord Hailsham.

[13180] Judges in appeal courts these days do not confine themselves to authorities from a particular jurisdiction. Read the reports
and you will find references to cases from what might have been
considered far flung places a generation or two ago. Now courts
can be influenced by the wisdom of Canada, the United Kingdom,
New Zealand – wherever wise judges can be found. It is a daunting
task to look up these cases and principles. But you will be before an
appeal court. None of your preparation of the law will be wasted.

[13185] If there is an important case against you, cite it. You will
have the chance to distinguish it, perhaps. If you don't refer to it,
your opponent will undermine your argument with it. But more
than that, the court will admire your honesty and decency and will
be more receptive to your arguments. A good reputation is worth
an immense amount. Courts know they can trust you.

[13190] Whatever you do, don't read out great slabs from a case. You
may have annexed a copy of the case to your written submissions. If
so, the judges will probably have read it. At most, cite the case and
the principle. If you do want to read from it, pick out the essence
contained in a sentence or two. You hope that the short reference
will tantalise them enough to prompt them to immerse themselves
in the detail of the case when they reserve.

Summary

[13195] In a careful and thorough article on appellate advocacy,[39]
Kirby J set out and explained the following ten points:

1. Know the court.
2. Know the law.
3. Use the opening.
4. Conceptualise the case.
5. Watch the bench.
6. Substance over elegance.
7. Cite authority with care.
8. Honesty at all times.
9. Courage under fire.
10. Explain policy and principle.

[13200] Appeals are demanding. Best of luck.

[39] Kirby J, "Ten rules of appellate advocacy" (1995) 69 ALJ 964.

Chapter 14

Legal writing

Introduction

[14000] Every lawyer does a lot of formal writing. It will usually be a submission to the court. Your writing must be accurate and persuasive. It is the preliminary and important part of advocacy. You don't want to run any risk of being misunderstood. A listener of spoken words may interpret them in a way that was not intended.[1] That may be conscious or unconscious. With written words, that risk should be reduced. The more accurate the writing, the lower the risk.

[14005] Courts are increasing their demand for written submissions. Courts of Appeal have practice directions to that effect. Not only that, but trial courts to a greater degree than ever before expect submissions in writing.[2] Your submissions on complex legal propositions to a trial court have a greater chance of success when they are in writing, supplemented by your spoken argument. Kirby J said:

> With the increase of workload of the courts, there is a growing pressure to commit more argument to writing. Thus it is more important today to recognise the special skills of written advocacy. On average, the written word can be read four times more quickly than the same word can be spoken.[3]

But keep your written submission as short as you can. The longer it is, the less likely is the judicial officer to read it and absorb it.[4]

[14010] This chapter is not designed to tell you what the content of your writing should be. For that you will need to look at the practice

---

[1] Often referred to as deriving from structuralism. See, for example, *Butera v DPP* (Vic) (1987) 164 CLR 180 at 209 per Gaudron J.

[2] Kirby J, "The future of appellate advocacy" (2006) 27 Aust Bar Rev 141 at 143.

[3] Kirby J, "Ten rules of appellate advocacy" (1995) 69 ALJ 964 at 975.

[4] Heydon J, "Reciprocal duties of Bench and Bar" (2007) 81 ALJ 23 at 31.

rules of the court to which you are directing your submissions. If you are appearing in an appeal court, it would be wise to ask the advice of Court of Appeal regulars about content, style and length of your submissions there.

[14015] Of course there is no fixed form of English. It is in a constant state of change. But subject to that, I hope to refresh the fundamentals of tried and true grammar, the use of simple words and something of style.

Preparation

[14020] A lawyer prepares a court case by doing a great amount of hard work. A submission calls for the same diligence.

[14025] Often a lawyer will do a good deal of writing in a draft. Many of us settle our thoughts by writing. We draft and redraft. But a draft is not the finished product. Hard work does not mean graceful writing. That is its own skill. Not all judges write well, although the industry is obvious.

[14030] The aim of any writing is to be easily understood. Even complex ideas can be expressed simply without being superficial or simplistic. W. Somerset Maugham said, "If you could write lucidly, simply, euphoniously and yet with liveliness you would write perfectly . . . A good style should show no sign of effort."[5]

[14035] But writing is not an easy business. There are some references on style that I keep close to hand. I find them a great help.[6]

Use the positive and the active voice

[14040] Use the positive and the active voice whenever you can. Lawyers are great ones for using negatives, and even double and triple negatives:

> I do not disagree with the conclusion that the Secretary of State is not an independent and impartial tribunal.[7]

[5] W. Somerset Maugham, *The Summing Up*, 1938, Heinemann, London.

[6] The first is an essay by George Orwell, "Politics and the English Language", 1946, Horizon, London. The second is W Strunk and EB White, *The Elements of Style*, 4th ed., 2000, Longman, New York. I also keep a thesaurus nearby; *Chambers* is more efficient than *Roget*.

[7] *Alconbury Developments Ltd v Secretary of State for the Environment, Transport and the Regions* [2003] 2 AC 295 at 339 [124] per Lord Hoffman.

The passive is in currency, too. Here is an example. In *Powell* the court examined whether a judge should specify the discount on sentence for a plea of guilty. The court said:

> The practice and policy with respect to identifying a discount for the matters referred to by the sentencing judge have not yet been shown to be wrong in principle by a binding decision of the High Court.[8]

One ordinary technique is to start the sentence with the subject. Perhaps the court could have said:

> The sentencing judge referred to the practice and policy for identifying the matters comprising a discount. The High Court has not given a binding decision showing that the principle is wrong.

Short sentences

[14045] There are many sentences in judgments that are festooned with riders, qualifications, exceptions, limitations and conditions.[9] My rule of thumb is to keep sentences short, with one issue in every sentence. That is the way we cross-examine. I apply the same principle to writing. In any event, no one sentence is likely to contain every qualification you may want in submissions on the law. Using short sentences also means you will not be confounded by the fancy rules of punctuation. Again, Kirby J said:

> The recent emphasis, in the written work of lawyers, upon the rules of plain English expression may also have its reflection in oral communication. Short sentences. Speaking in the active voice. Avoid circumlocution and clichés. These rules are as important to the advocate as to the drafter.[10]

Simple words

[14050] You can often use a short simple word instead of a complex one. Aitken said, "[A]rchaic language should be replaced by words in current use, unless its retention serves a useful purpose."[11] Here are some examples:

---

8   *R v Powell* (2001) 81 SASR 9 (CCA) at 14 [24] per Prior J.
9   A prime example is Cotton LJ in *North London Railway Co v Great North Railway Co* (1883) 11 QBD 30 at 39.
10 Kirby J, "Ten rules of appellate advocacy" (1995) 69 ALJ 964 at 965.
11 J K Aitken, *Elements of Drafting*, 4th ed., 1968, Law Book Co, Sydney, pp. 3–4.

advert	refer
adumbrate	foreshadow
commence	start, begin
curtail	lessen, shorten
desire	wish, want
endeavour	try
locality	place
locate	find
proceed	go
purchase	buy
purport (verb)	claim, suggest
purport (noun)	meaning, spirit
pursuant to	because of, according to, under
render	make
require	want, need
reside	live
residence	home
Socratic dialogue	debate

[14055] Avoid complex words and constructions. Do not follow the example of Jenkinson J:

> The etiolation of delictual colour in s.32(1) derives ... not only from the merger of the tortious liability in a judgment or from extinction of the tortious cause of action by payment of a claim, satisfaction of either of which gives rise to the cause of action created by the sub-section, but also from the use in the sub-section of the phrase "as a debt".[12]

Dependent clauses and participial phrases

[14060] Do not start a sentence with a dependent clause beginning with *that*. We never speak in that way but some lawyers and judges have acquired that habit in their writing. It is hard to understand. It even looks artificial. Consider this sentence by Gummow J:

> That a particular constitutional doctrine requires close attention to the detail of the impugned legislation and that its invalidating effect may be demonstrated infrequently does not, as the history of *Melbourne Corporation* over 50 years shows, warrant its description at any one time as a dead letter.[13]

[12] *Ryder v Hartford Insurance Co* [1977] VR 257 at 266 (Jenkinson J).
[13] *Fardon v Attorney-General* (Qld) (2004) 223 CLR 575 at 618 [104] per Gummow J.

[14065] If you must start a sentence with a participial phrase, make sure that the phrase refers to the subject. Here is an example:

Arriving late in chambers, the conference was delayed by the client.

The conference did not arrive late. The client did. Try changing the sentence to the active. It improves things a little but does not remove the clumsiness:

Arriving late in chambers, the client delayed the conference.

The following bizarre example should point up the difficulty with this form of writing:

Being time-worn, the advocate made a low offer for the wig.

Digraphs

[14070] The term "digraph" means two letters that stand for one sound. Examples are *gh* as in *tough*, *sh* as in *dash* and so on. At one time the vowels *a* and *e* were joined: *æ*. This is known as a ligature. *Chimæra* is an example. Sometimes *o* and *e* were joined, as in *amœba*. Some of these spellings are quietly falling into disuse. *Encyclopædia* is gradually becoming *encyclopedia*[14] and *chimæra* is *chimera*.[15] But some remain, at least for the moment, especially in medical terms such as *amoeba*, *anaemia* and *haemorrhage*. In medical circles, there is much debate over *pediatrics* versus *paediatrics*. So take care to check the correct spelling, and use the version that your audience favours.

The subjunctive

[14075] Like people, verbs have moods. Two of them are the indicative and the subjunctive. We use the indicative form to make factual statements:

I am here.

In earlier days, people used the subjunctive to express wishes or desires:

If I were here . . .

---

[14] *Randwick Corporation v Rutledge* (1959) 102 CLR 54 at 82–83 per Windeyer J.
[15] *Thomas v The Queen* (1960) 102 CLR 584 at 605 per Windeyer J.

The subjunctive has fallen from regular use, although we still see it in some commonly used expressions: *If need be, Come what may, Be that as it may, Far be it from me, If I were you, As it were.*

It is also familiar in some well-known words:

> If music be the food of love play on . . .[16]
> If I were a rich man . . .[17]

You may care to revive the use of the subjunctive, particularly after the word *if*. Here is an example of the correct use of the subjunctive followed by the indicative:

> If the jury were persuaded that Brien was guilty of manslaughter . . .[18]

Personal pronouns and prepositions

[14080] Personal pronouns and the relative pronoun *who* change from nominative to objective case. They also have separate forms for the possessive case.

Nominative	Objective	Possessive
I	me	my
he	him	his
she	her	hers
we	us	our
they	them	their
who	whom	whose

Prepositions take the objective case. Here are some common examples using the prepositions *to* and *between*:

> The cleaner spoke to him and me. (NOT The cleaner spoke to he and I.)

> Between you and me . . . (NOT Between you and I . . .)

Thus it was incorrect grammar for counsel to have said, "This has been the subject of a heated exchange between your Honour and I."[19] It should have been "between your Honour and me".

[14085] Other prepositions are used with words of contrast: similar *to*; identical *with*. *Compare* takes the prepositions *to* or *with*. Using

---

[16] The starting words of Shakespeare's *Twelfth Night*.
[17] Well-known start of the lyrics of the song in *Fiddler on the Roof*.
[18] *R v Wood & Ors* (1996) 87 A Crim R 346 (Qld CA) at 354 per Macrossan CJ.
[19] *R v Howes* (2000) 2 VR 141 at 147 [15] per Winneke P.

compare to is to point out something essentially different, while *compare with* is to point to a difference of something of the same type:

> A court case may be compared to polite warfare.

> The Australian High Court may be compared with the US Supreme Court.

Gender neutrality

[14090] In days long gone, a lot of writing was expressed in the masculine singular:

> If a person has been convicted he has a right to appeal.

The excuse was that under the *Interpretation Acts* the masculine included the feminine. That style of writing has long since passed and rightly so. The main question is how to write with style and be gender neutral? *He or she, him or her* is polite but clumsy. You don't always have to use them and still be respectful. The main trick is to redraft using a little imagination. In *York*, McHugh J referred to:

> . . . a grave risk that fellow prisoners will kill the convicted person while he or she is in custody.[20]

His Honour could have said:

> that fellow prisoners will kill the convicted person in custody OR that fellow prisoners will kill the convicted person while that person is in custody.

In *Bajic* Byrne J said:

> . . . it is not proper for a prosecutor to cross-examine an accused inviting him or her to speculate as to any motive for a Crown witness to lie.[21]

His Honour could have said:

> . . . it is not proper for a prosecutor to cross-examine an accused inviting speculation on any motive for a prosecution witness to lie.

[14095] So you can see that the first method of not using *he and she* is to redraft. There is another technique. You can change the sentence to *they* and *their* (third person plural) or even to *you* and *your* (second person singular).

---

[20] *York v The Queen* (2005) 225 CLR 466 at 470 [10].
[21] *R v Bajic* (2005) 154 A Crim R 196 at 217 [109].

An advocate does his or her best to defend the case as well as he or she can.

Change to:

Advocates do their best to defend cases as well as they can. OR
As an advocate you do your best to defend the case as well as you can.

[14100] Some strictly feminine words survive in the law. The feminine of *executor* is *executrix* and of *testator*, *testatrix*. The word *prosecutrix* is still sometimes used to describe a female complainant in a sex case.[22]

[14105] Neutrality is not confined to gender. Your writing must also be sensitive to race, religion, ethnicity and sexuality.

The gerund

[14110] A gerund is a verb used as a noun.[23] A gerund ends in -*ing*.

Seeing is believing.

For the most part a gerund takes the possessive, just as a noun does.

I was worried about his arriving late at court. (The gerund is *arriving*.)

Defence counsel was pleased by the judge's finding that there was no case to answer.

They were sad at my losing the case.

I objected to their giving evidence.

You must use the possessive when the gerund is the subject of the sentence.

My singing in the final address surprised them all.

Use words correctly

[14115] Be careful to give words their proper meanings. Here are some example of words and their present usage.

---

[22] See, for example, *Re Minister for Immigration and Multicultural Affairs; Ex parte S154* (2003) 77 ALJR 1909; *R v Carroll* (2002) 213 CLR 635 at 663 [91] per Gaudron and Gummow JJ.

[23] Every book on grammar spends a lot of time on the gerund.

condign This word means well deserved, especially of punishment. Courts often use it wrongly to mean severe.[24]

fulsome Of flattery this adjective means so gross as to be disgustingly fawning because of its excess. In very recent times *fulsome praise* has been used to mean extremely complimentary. In other settings it means complete or full.[25] So take care before using the word.

hopefully This is a useful adverb. It means with hope or in a hopeful manner. However, people often use it as an adverb to start a sentence, meaning "I hope".[26] So when advocates say "Hopefully, I'll be ready for court", they really mean "I hope that I'll be ready for court". I prefer traditional usage. If you mean "I hope", say so, and write it that way. Use *hopefully* only as an adverb of manner, as in "I went to court hopefully", meaning "I went to court feeling hopeful."

infer and *imply* Sometimes you will hear them wrongly used as synonyms. *Infer* means to draw a conclusion. *Imply* means to insinuate, to hint.

might and *may* These can both be used for present and for future time, with *might* suggesting a lower probability:

My case may be listed for next Tuesday.

I might get a brief in the appeal; time will tell.

sanction This word has two opposite meanings. One is a penalty for not observing the law. The other meaning is the reward for observing the law. Make sure to use the meaning you intend.[27]

substantial and *substantive* Don't mix these adjectives. *Substantial* means essential, ample, solidly based. *Substantive* in the legal

---

[24] See, for example, *Veen v The Queen* (1988) 164 CLR 465 at 477 per Mason CJ, Brennan, Dawson and Toohey JJ; *R v Solomon* (2005) 153 A Crim R 32 at 37 [19] (NSW CCA). There are many others.

[25] See, for example, *Walsh v Law Society of New South Wales* (1999) 198 CLR 73 at 88 [44] per McHugh, Kirby and Callinan JJ.

[26] See, for example, *Deputy Commissioner of Taxation v Richard Walter Pty Ltd* (1995) 183 CLR 168 at 205 per Deane and Gaudron JJ.

[27] There are a few such words sometimes called contronyms or auto-antonyms. Another is *cleave*. It means to split apart. It also means to join together. "Therefore shall a man leave his father and his mother, and shall cleave unto his wife": Bible Genesis 2.24. Another could be *oversight*.

setting generally means statutory, depending on the written law for its authority.

uninterested and *disinterested* These have quite different meanings. *Uninterested* means lacking concern. *Disinterested* means impartial:

> He was completely uninterested in my problems. (He couldn't care less.)

> A judge is expected to be disinterested (totally impartial).

Plurals

[14120] I want to deal here only with a few plurals of unusual words, particularly those that come from Greek or Latin. Make sure you use the correct plural form. Check a reference if you are in any doubt.

Singular	Plural
addendum	addenda
analysis	analyses
appendix	appendices (usage is changing to appendixes)
bacterium	bacteria
crisis	crises
criterion	criteria
datum	data
executrix	executrices
formula	formulae
index	indices (usage is changing to indexes)
medium	media
memorandum	memoranda
moratorium	moratoria
phenomenon	phenomena
referendum	referenda (usage is changing to referendums)
sanatorium	sanatoria (usage is changing to sanitoriums)
stratum	strata
synthesis	syntheses

Verbs

[14125] The words *either* and *neither*, *everybody* and *nobody* take a singular verb. So do *none* and *each*.

> Each piece of evidence was circumstantial, but none was conclusive.

Everybody at the Bar claims to be a proficient advocate.

Nobody was charged with an offence though everyone at the house was a suspect.

[14130] An infinitive verb is the form that has *to* before it:

To err is human, to forgive, divine.[28]

To sleep: perchance to dream.[29]

You split the infinitive by putting a word, usually an adverb, between *to* and the verb:

It was hard to really enjoy being in that court.

In the past, grammarians frowned on the split infinitive. Those days are long gone. The form can even be useful now and again. But I try to avoid the split infinitive in my writing. It is not just my pedantry. My main reason is that if I write a submission to a court, the last thing I want is a judge with a traditional eye for grammar being distracted by abhorrence for the split infinitive. It's easy to avoid splitting the infinitive. Consider the following split infinitive:

The advocate failed to fully observe the rule in *Browne v Dunn*.

You can simply shift the word *fully*. It can go before the infinitive, after the infinitive or at the end of the sentence. There is a subtle difference of meaning between the sentences depending on where you put the adverb.

The advocate failed fully to observe the rule in *Browne v Dunn*.
The advocate failed to observe fully the rule in *Browne v Dunn*.
The advocate failed to observe the rule in *Browne v Dunn* fully.

Do not create a clumsy sentence in order to avoid splitting an infinitive. This may distract even a pedantic reader. Choose the most natural-sounding way of expressing your meaning.

Numbers

[14135] When you are writing numerals, use words for the numbers one to nine. From 10 onwards use figures. Never start a sentence with a figure. If you need to use adverbs for numbering, I recommend

---

[28] Alexander Pope, *Essay on Criticism*, 1711, line 525.
[29] William Shakespeare, *Hamlet*, Act 3, scene 1, line 65.

using first, second, third and so on, rather than firstly, secondly, thirdly.

Less and *fewer*. *Less* applies to a reduced quantity. *Fewer* applies to a reduced number:

> Fewer than 20 judges sat that year.

> The court hears fewer appeals in January than in any other month.

> One of the judges did far less work than the others.

> He decided that he should put less butter on his toast.

> As the years go on I find that I am smoking my pipe less.

Comparatives

[14140] Adjectives allow us to compare one thing with another. The comparative adjective allows us to compare two things.

> The first brief was long, but this is longer.

The superlative form describes the highest kind or order.

> This is the longest brief I've ever read.

The comparative form is falling out of use in ordinary conversation. You will often hear a parent of two children say something like "my youngest child is the best behaved". If you need to compare in your writing, use the comparative. In most cases, the comparative is formed by adding -*er*:

Positive	Comparative	Superlative
fine	finer	finest
young	younger	youngest
old	older	oldest

The adjectives that are heavily worked have their own forms:

good	better	best
bad	worse	worst

An adjective with three or more syllables usually has a word added:

expansive	more expansive	most expansive
substantial	more substantial	most substantial

So make sure that your writing uses the proper form of adjective when you need to compare.

In a singles tennis match, the player with the better serve is more likely to win.

A fine example of the use of the comparative and superlative is the inscription from the Furphy water cart[30]:

Good, better, best – never let it rest,
Until your good is better, and your better best.

Politeness

[14145] Pay a person respect.[31] Use the titles *Mr, Mrs, Ms* and even the unpopular *Miss*. Kirby J is polite in court and in his judgments. He always uses these titles.

[14150] A usage that rankles with me is the word *one* to describe a person who is not a central character. I have never heard ordinary people describe another person that way but it intrudes its ungraceful rudeness into judgments.

The applicant was presented . . . with one Jones . . .[32]

. . . evidence was led from the owner of this property (one Smith) . . .[33]

The business was conducted by two principals, one Williams and the applicant.[34]

It would have been easy enough to refer to Mr Jones, Mr Smith, Mr Williams.

Pleonasm

[14155] Avoid the pleonasm: the repetition of unnecessary words. Judges seem to use the pleonasm quite often. Here are some of them:

4 am in the morning[35]

I would remit the matter back to the District Court.[36]

---

[30] John Furphy invented and manufactured the Furphy water cart. The first one was built between 1878 and 1880 in Shepparton, Victoria. In 1895, he added this inscription to the plaque on each cart.
[31] In Chapter 3 [3110], I made the same point about politeness in asking questions.
[32] *R v Tierney* (1990) 51 A Crim R 446 (Vic CCA).
[33] *R v Kotzmann* (No 2) (2002) 128 A Crim R 479 at 489 [21] (Vic CA).
[34] *R v Hoad* (1989) 42 A Crim R 312 at 313 (Qld CCA).
[35] *R v Rugari* (2001) 122 A Crim R 1 at 3 [13].
[36] *R v Brownlow* (2003) 86 SASR 114 (CCA) at [62] per Sulan J.

ATM machine[37]

PIN number[38]

safe haven[39]

Even Sir Owen Dixon found himself "looking back in retrospect".[40]

Other languages

[14160] Avoid other languages if you can. Some Latin may be necessary such as *habeas corpus*, an action *in rem* and *mens rea*. Avoid quoting extensively from ancient Latin or Greek. Kirby J made an extensive reference to ancient Greek in one of his judgments.[41] It may be stylish in a judgment, but it would be a meaningless distraction in a submission.

Padding

[14165] Strunk and White describe the phrase *in terms of* as "a piece of padding best omitted".[42] The same would apply to *with regard to* and *in relation to*. If you don't redraft completely, simple words such as *on, about, over, of* or *because* can replace them. Consider these examples, which I take from judgments, and their simpler versions following:

> I regard it as inappropriate to speak in terms of waiver in relation to the claim book.[43]

> There was indeed no dispute with regard to the factual issues . . .[44]

> It was proper to charge the jury in terms of the reasonable possibilities having regard to the onus of proof borne by the Crown.[45]

> [C]ommittal proceedings in relation to the applicant commenced."[46]

---

[37] *R v Newton* (2002) 128 A Crim R 185 (SA CCA) at [3] per Perry J.

[38] *R v Lewis* (2003) 142 A Crim R 254 (NSW CCA) at 256 [8]-[10] per Howie J.

[39] *R v Calder* [1987] 1 Qd R 62 (CCA) at 64 per Connolly J.

[40] Sir Owen Dixon (1955) 29 ALJ 272.

[41] *Graham Barclay Oysters Pty Ltd v Ryan* (2002) 211 CLR 540 at 616 [211].

[42] Strunk and White, *The Elements of Style*, 4th ed., 2000, Longman, New York, p. 50.

[43] *Attorney-General (NT) v Maurice* (1986) 161 CLR 475 at 495 per Dawson J.

[44] *R v Minani* (2005) 154 A Crim R 347 (NSW CCA) at 356 [30] per Hunt AJA.

[45] *R v KJ* (2005) 154 A Crim R 139 (Vic CA) at 143 [21] per Osborn AJA.

[46] *R v Nicholas* (2000) 111 A Crim R 490 at 493 [5] (Vic CA)

These words may have been better expressed as:

> I regard it as inappropriate to speak of waiver about the claim book.

> There was indeed no dispute about factual issues . . .

> It was proper to charge the jury on the reasonable possibilities because of the onus of proof borne by the Crown.

> [T]he applicant's committal started.

[14170] Worse still, there is any amount of legislation that now contains *with regard to*. Courts have to grapple with the meaning.

Overworked metaphors

[14175] Be wary of using corny metaphors: *cool, calm and collected, weird and wonderful, not in any way, shape or form*. There are many others: *the bottom line, at the end of the day, the worst-case scenario, low profile*. Nor should you import American baseball expressions: *out of left field, in the ball park, line ball, step up to the plate*. Your writing will be carefully designed to achieve your purpose. Don't use a metaphor unless your ear tells you that it is exactly right for the point you want to make.[47]

Sayings

[14180] If you must use sayings, use them correctly. All that *glisters* is not gold. The lily is *painted*. A little *learning* is a dangerous thing. All the *schemes* of mice and men. The *love of* money is the root of all evil. When at Rome do as *Rome does*. One *fell* swoop. Short *shrift*.

Authorised reports

[14185] Authorised reports are those that have been approved by the judges.[48] When you cite a case in your writing, cite the authorised report if it appears there. Currently, when a case is on the internet, there is rarely a change between that and how the case appears in the authorised report. But there were quite a few changes in earlier times.

---

[47] Michael Meehan, "The Good, the Bad and the Ugly: Judicial Literacy and the Australian Cultural Cringe" (1990) 12 Adel LR 431, wrote (at 436) "Allusion is often just the employment of the 'apt phrase', the piquant aphorism, or the dash of contextual colour."

[48] David Ross QC, *Ross on Crime*, 3rd ed., 2007, Lawbook Co, Sydney, Appendix E: Authorised Reports.

[14190] The best example I know of a substantial change is *R v Morris*. In the early report of the case, [1950] 1 All ER 965 at 966 and 34 Cr App 210 at 212–213, Lord Goddard set out the history of the law on punishment for common law offences. That would have been how the judgment was delivered. But when you look at the authorised report of the case at [1951] 1 KB 394 at 395–396 you can see that his Lordship had worked on the case again and totally recast the propositions.

[14195] There is only one set of authorised reports for each jurisdiction at any one time.

[14200] When you refer to the year of the case, quote the year of its being decided, not the year on the outside of the law report. So *Putland v The Queen* is (2004) 218 CLR 174, even though it appears in the CLR volume with 2003–2004 on its spine. The decision was handed down in 2004, so that is the year to cite.

[14205] Square brackets or round? Use round brackets for reports from all jurisdictions in Australia except Queensland, which has the year of the report in square brackets. You need the square brackets when the year is the only clue on where to find the case in the volumes of the reports. In New Zealand and now in England all the reports use square brackets.

The start

[14210] Beware of starting your submission in the style of a short story. With some judges it is having a revival. Denning LJ was a great fan of the style. Here are some examples:

> In summer time village cricket is the delight of everyone. Nearly every village has its own cricket field where the old men play and the young men watch.[49]

> It happened on 19 April 1964. It was bluebell time in Kent.[50]

> This is the case of the barmaid who was badly bitten by the big dog.[51]

It may be right for a judge, but I doubt it. It tends towards the trivial. So whatever you do, don't use it in a submission.

---

[49] *Miller v Jackson* [1977] 1 QB 966 at 976.
[50] *Hinz v Berry* [1970] 2 QB 40 at 42.
[51] *Cummings v Granger* [1977] QB 397 at 402.

[14215] These opening words have proliferated a fashion. In 1999 in Victoria, Cummins J gave judgment in a contempt of court case. He started this way:

> The hills south of Yarragon are green and shaded. The hourglass of the Latrobe Valley is there at its most slender . . .[52]

Queensland Bar News described the judgment as Denning-esque.[53]

[14220] In my submissions I like to begin with the central question and the answer. McHugh J started his later judgments in the High Court that way. His Honour raised this style of opening to an art form in *Stevens*:

> This appeal, which arises out of a conviction for murder in the Supreme Court of Queensland, must be allowed because the trial judge refused to direct the jury to determine whether the deceased died as a result of an accident.[54]

[14225] Southwood J has followed suit beautifully:

> The appellant was convicted . . . of aggravated assault . . . after it was found by the presiding magistrate that she had urged her family dog to bite the victim and the dog had bitten the victim accordingly. She appeals against her conviction for the circumstance of aggravation of threaten with an offensive weapon – her dog.
>
> The principal question in this appeal is whether a dog is an "article" within the definition of "offensive weapon". In my opinion a dog is not an "article" and the appeal should be allowed.[55]

[14230] Every writer of a journal article knows all about starting with a summary. Editors demand it.

Quotations

[14235] Avoid long quotations from judgments. We have all read those judgments that contain interminable extracts of what judges have said in other cases. The best judgments are those that set out the principles, and footnote the source of each.

---

[52] *Anissa Pty Ltd v Parsons* [1999] VSC 430 (8 November 1999).
[53] *Queensland Bar News*, December 2003, p. 18.
[54] *Stevens v The Queen* (2005) 80 ALJR 91; 222 ALR 40 at [21].
[55] *Tomlins v Brennan* (2006) 18 NTLR 80 at 98 [72]–[73].

[14240] The same principle applies to your written submissions to a court. Set out the proposition. Footnote the source. As a general rule, you should never need more than three authorities for any one submission.

[14245] As to quotation marks, use them only when truly quoting. Occasionally you may want to use an unusual or colloquial phrase. If your ear tells you that it is right, use it. But whatever you do, don't put it in quotation marks. The best judges never do. In *Koutsouridis*, Fullagar J said that not taking points at trial and keeping them for appeal might allow two bites of the cherry.[56] In England, Collins J allowed an appeal. His Honour's conclusion was that the claimant had not had a fair crack of the whip.[57] In the House of Lords, Lord Griffiths said of the application of abuse of process to the facts of the case that it was a horse of a very different colour.[58] In NSW District Court Judge Geraghty said, "Security is like love; like ice-cream; like peace; like praise – one can never get enough of it."[59] The judges did not put these unusual expressions in quotation marks and neither should you.

Summary

[14250] Writing is an art. Legal writing may have a different quality when you are trying to fit your words to express the law and your argument. It's definitely not fiction, and the rules that guide fiction writers are quite distinct from ours.

[14255] With computers it is easy to write and correct and then rewrite. Use simple words. Keep the sentences short. Use the active and singular wherever possible. Use the tools of grammar and avoid the snags as best you can. Make the words do what you expect of them. Be like the best lawyers who do draft after draft until the whole piece is tickety-boo.

---

[56] *R v Koutsouridis* (1982) 7 A Crim R 237 (Vic CCA) at 242 per Fullagar J.

[57] *R (on the application of Lynch) v General Dental Council* [2004] 1 All ER 1159 at 1171 [38].

[58] *R v Horseferry Road Magistrates' Court; Ex parte Bennett* [1994] 1 AC 42 at 64.

[59] Quoted by Mason P on the appeal: *English v Rogers* [2005] NSWCA 327 (21 September 2005) at [44]. (It was the quote of the month in (2006) 80 ALJ 7 at 11.)

Chapter 15

Etiquette and ethics

Introduction

[15000] Throughout the book I have referred to ethics and etiquette. In this last chapter I will simply list the responsibilities of an advocate without further comment. If you are in doubt about any matter in a case, consult the ethics committee of your Bar or Law Society.

Parties and witnesses

[15005]

1. If you act for more than one party, you risk a conflict of interest.
2. Some Bars allow you to see the client and the witnesses, and some not. If you do see them, have someone else present, speak to them one by one, suggest no line and do not say what another witness has told you.

Before court

[15010]

3. Send the court and your opponent any written submissions.
4. Send the court and your opponent any list of authorities and a copy of any unreported judgment on which you rely. Always cite the authorised reports.
5. Make sure you have all of the papers you need.
6. Dress properly, either in robes or conservative formal dress.
7. Arrange to be on time.
8. Do not talk to the judge alone about the case.
9. If you negotiate with your opponent, make a note of it.
10. Draft possible orders.

In court before your case is heard
[15015]

11. Observe the courtesy of the Bar table. Those senior to you will have the seats and will mention their cases before yours.
12. Do not speak or move when a witness is being sworn or affirmed.
13. Speak quietly and only if necessary. Better still, pass a note.
14. Negotiate with your opponent outside court.
15. Switch off mobile phones.
16. Do not carry newspapers unless necessary for your case.
17. Do not let the Bar table be vacant when the judge is still sitting.
18. Tell the court as soon as your case is settled.

During your case
[15020]

19. Arrange for witnesses producing documents to be called early.
20. Try not to keep witnesses waiting.
21. Open your case truly.
22. You must not lead evidence that you know to be false.
23. In cross-examination you must not suggest matters you know to be false.
24. You must never mislead the court.
25. Speak from the Bar table.
26. Approach the witness only by leave.
27. Stand when speaking or when the judge is speaking to you.
28. Sit when your opponent is making an objection.
29. Do not talk over the top of anyone, particularly the judge.
30. Do not display a prejudicial document in the sight of the jury.
31. Refer to the judge by proper title: "Your Lordship", "Your Honour".
32. Never express a personal opinion. Advocates make submissions.
33. Do not thank the judge other than for a rare personal favour. Say, "If Your Honour pleases".
34. Respect the judge and the judge's position. Never be patronising or familiar.
35. Be polite to all and maintain your composure.
36. Maintain a respectful posture. Do not lounge.

37. Use humour sparingly and only to advance your case. Never tell jokes.
38. Do not speak privately to your witness during cross-examination without your opponent's prior approval.
39. In your final address, you must not refer to evidence that has not been given.

After the case
[15025]

40. Do not tell your opponent about the defects in the case you have settled. You might never settle another one again.
41. Be gracious in victory and in defeat.

Index

Abalos v Australian Postal Commission
(1990) 171 CLR 167, **143**
Aboriginal witnesses, **29**
abuse of process submission, **116**
accused
referring to, **28**
active voice, **148**
Adams, John Bodkin, **94**
address of witness, ascertaining, **39**
addressing the court, **119**
admissible evidence, 4, 108
see evidence
admissions, **21**
adverse answers
repeating, **33**
advocacy
nature of, **1**
advocates
obligations of, **1**, **9**
qualities of, **1**
age effect on sentencing, **134**
Ahern v The Queen (1988) 165 CLR 87,
8
aims of cross-examination, **49**
Ajodha v The State [1982] AC 204,
114
Alchin v Commissioner for Railways
(1935) 35 SR (NSW) FC 498,
88, 89, 97, 98
Alexander v Manley (2004) 29 WAR
194, **90, 98**
Al-Hashimi v The Queen (2004) 181
FLR 383, **56**
Alister v The Queen (1984) 154 CLR
404, **98**

Allied Pastoral Holdings v FCT [1983]
1 NSWLR 1, **52**
analysis for appeals, **140**
Anissa Pty Ltd v Parsons [1999] VSC
430, **163**
antecedents, **132**
appeals, **137**
grounds for, **22, 136**
arguing with witnesses, **30**
Arthur JS Hall v Simons [2002] 1 AC
615, **9**
Attorney-General (NT) v Maurice
(1986) 161 CLR 475, **99, 160**
*Attorney-General's Reference (No 3 of
1994)* [1998] AC 245, **139**
Attwood v The Queen (1960) 102 CLR
353, **46**
*Australian Safeway Stores Pty Ltd v
Zaluzna* (1987) 162 CLR 479,
110
authorised reports, **161**

bad reputation, **72**
Bajic case, **153**
Barker, Ian, **121, 124**
barristers, 1
see advocates
Basha inquiry, **19, 114**
Beevis v Dawson [1957] 1 QB 195, **35**
behaviour, **8, 166**
Bell v The Queen (1985) 7 FCR 555, **72**
Bench, 9
see judges
Benedetto v The Queen [2003] 1 WLR
1545, **27, 120, 143**

biased experts, **85**
Bolster rule, **38**
books, learning from, **7**
brackets in legal writing, **162**
*Brian Gardner Motors Pty Ltd v
        Bembridge* (2000) 120 A Crim R
        53, **114**
briefs, handling of, **13**
Browne v Dunn (1893) 6 R 67, **20**, **51**,
        80
Bryan, William Jennings, **34**
Bugg v Day (1949) 79 CLR 442, **71**
Bull v The Queen (2000) 201 CLR 443,
        94
Bulstrode v Trimble [1970] VR 840, **52**
Burnell v British Transport Commission
        [1956] 1 QB 187, **99**
Butera v DPP (Vic) (1987) 164 CLR
        180, **14**, **15**, **147**
Byrne J, **153**
Byrne v Godfree (1997) 96 A Crim R
        197, **22**
Byrnes v The Queen (1999) 199 CLR 1,
        138

cab rank rule, 9
Cadbury v Daily News, **64**, **102**
calling for a document, **89**
Campbell, Don, **59**
Carson, Edward, **17**, **61**
*Carter v Northmore Hale Davy and
        Leake* (1995) 183 CLR 121, **108**
case concept, **12**
Case Stated by DPP (No 1 of 1993)
        (1993) 66 A Crim R 259, **55**
case stated procedure, **139**
cases
        ethical conduct of, **166**
        index of, **13**
        materials for, **16**
        proof of, **36**
        won on admissible evidence, **4**
        work during, **22**
Cassell & Co v Broome [1972] AC 1027,
        145
Chamberlain case, **121**, **124**, **125**
charts, **15**, **120**

Chayna, Andre, **82**
        see R v Chayna (1993) 66 A Crim R
                178
Cheney v The Queen (1991) 28 FCR
        103, **92**
children as witnesses, **20**, **73**
Chong & Toh v R (1989) 40 A Crim R
        22, **34**
chronological order for evidence, **42**
circumstantial evidence, **68**, **112**
civil cases
        opening addresses, **120**
        pre-trial documents, **23**
        steps in, **17**
civilian witnesses, **24**
Cleveland Report, **21**
clients
        obligations to, **9**, **165**
        referring to in court, **28**
closing addresses, **122**
closing the gates, **58**, **94**
Clyne v NSW Bar Association (1960)
        104 CLR 186, **1**
Collins J, **164**
*Collins v State Rail Authority of New
        South Wales* (1986) 5 NSWLR
        209 (CA), **140**
Collins, R.B., **80**
comments on evidence, **33**
comparatives, correct use of, **158**
complaints about procedure, **141**
concept of the case, **12**
confession, misleading statements as
        to, **27**
confrontation, **60**
contemporary notes, failure to consult,
        85
contradictions, addressing, **80**
Copeland v Smith [2000] 1 WLR 1371, **11**
Corkery, Michael, **122**
counsel, **6**
        see advocates
courage, need for, **3**
courtesy, **9**
        in demeanour, **35**
        in legal writing, **159**
        in stopping witnesses, **41**

courts
appeal powers, **139**
appeal practice, **143**
behaviour in, 8, **166**
lower, advocacy in, **6**
preparation for, 11, **165**
Cowan v Council of the City of Greater Wollongong (1954) 54 SR (NSW), **143**
credit of witnesses, **17**
not an issue in examination-in-chief, **38**
reviving, **106**
undermining, **50**, **54**
criminal cases
good character in, **46**
impact on victims, **133**
opening addresses, **120**
proof in, **110**
Criminal Procedure Act 1865, **88**
Crippen, Hawley Harvey, **18**, **69**
Cross, Sir Rupert, **19**
cross-examination, **48**
leading questions in, **31**
method and style, **60**
of experts, **76**
of hostile witnesses, **27**
on documents, **87**
preparing, **20**
re-examination arising from, **102**
Cummings v Granger [1977] QB 397, **162**
Cummins J, **163**
Cussen J, **28**
cutting off escape, **94**

damage control, advocacy as, **5**
damaging details, **62**
Darrow, Clarence, **4**, **34**, **86**, **123**
De Gruchy v The Queen (2002) 211 CLR 85, **112**
De Jesus v The Queen (1986) 61 ALJR 1, **4**
defence
closing address, **124**
witnesses for, **36**

demeanour
of advocate, **35**
of witnesses, **24**
Denning, Lord, **46**, **162**
denying an allegation, **37**
dependent clauses, **150**
Deputy Commissioner of Taxation v Richard Walter Pty Ltd (1995) 183 CLR 168, **155**
detail, level of, **37**
details, damaging, **62**
diagrams, **15**
diaries kept by police, **44**
Dietrich v The Queen (1992) 177 CLR 192, **116**
digraphs, **151**
directing a witness, **37**, **103**
Director of Public Prosecutions, **131**
Director of Public Prosecutions (No 1 of 1999) (1999) 8 NTLR 148, **140**
Director of Public Prosecutions (NT) v WJI (2004) 219 CLR 43, **111**
Director of Public Prosecutions v Kilbourne [1973] AC 729, **108**, **109**
documents 8, **16**
see also legal writing
assembly of, **13**
cross-examining on, **87**
re-examining on, **106**
should never be marked, **13**
Doggett v The Queen (2001) 208 CLR 343, **4**
D'Orta-Ekenaike v Victoria Legal Aid (2005) 233 CLR 1, **1**, **9**, **145**
DPP v Boardman [1975] AC 421, **109**
DPP v Grabovac [1998] 1 VR 664, **134**
DPP v Kilbourne [1973] AC 729, **114**
DPP v Sarosi (2000) 110 A Crim R 376, **10**
DPP v Stonehouse [1978] AC 55, **122**
drafting grounds for appeal, **141**
drawings, **15**
dress code, **165**
duties of an advocate, **9**

Eastman v The Queen (2000) 203 CLR 1, **143**

Ebatarinja v Price (1997) 137 FLR 281,
 139
effect of crime on victims, **133**
elements of cause of action or charge,
 18, **50**
emotions, use of, **3**
English, **27**
 see also language, use of
 simple, **27**, **41**, **149**
English v Rogers [2005] NSWCA 327,
 164
essence of advocacy, **1**
ethics, **8**, **165**
etiquette, **58**, **165**
 see also courtesy
even temper, **35**
 see also demeanour
events, index of, **14**
evidence
 admissibility of, **108**
 approach to, **14**
 bearing on each element, **18**
 cases won on, **4**
 chronological order of, **42**
 circumstantial, **68**, **116**
 fresh, in appeals, **143**
 important items not tested, **83**
 making comments on, **33**
 objections to, **113**
 rules of, **117**
 variations in, **45**
 witness statements, **23**
Evidence Act (NT), **88**
Evidence Act 1872 (Bangladesh), **88**
Evidence Act 1906 (WA), **88**
Evidence Act 1908 (New Zealand), **88**
Evidence Act 1929 (SA), **88**
Evidence Act 1950 (Malaysia), **88**
Evidence Act 1958 (Vic), **88**
Evidence Act 1971 (ACT), **88**
Evidence Act 1977 (Qld), **88**
Evidence Act 1985 (Canada), **88**
Evidence Act 1995 (Cth), **27**, **31**
Evidence Act 1995 (NSW), **27**, **31**
Evidence Act 2001 (Tas), **27**, **31**
Evidence Acts, **88**
evidence-in-chief, **46**
 see examination-in-chief

examination-in-chief, **36**
examples, use of, **126**
exhibits
 examining, **17**
 index of, **14**
experience and logic test, **109**
expert witnesses **23**, **25**
 see also opinion evidence
 in closing address, **125**
 cross-examination of, **76**
 introducing, **39**
 language used by, **28**
 order of questions, **43**
 to psychological impairment, **133**
eye contact, **38**

facts
 admissions of, **21**
 agreement on, **132**
 already found, **142**
 cross-examination on, **51**
 evidence vs., **4**
 in issue, **109**
 in pleas in mitigation, **135**
falsehoods, **26**
 see misleading statements
Fardon v Attorney-General (Qld)
 (2004) 223 CLR 575, **150**
feminine words surviving in law, **154**
final address, **22**
Financial Wisdom Ltd v Newman
 (2005) 12 VR 79, **141**
Fitzgibbon, Daniel, **102**
Fitzpatrick v Walter E Cooper Pty Ltd
 (1935) 54 CLR 200, **69**
Fitzpatrick, Mrs, **69**
forms of question, **40**, **55**, **115**
Fox v Percy (2003) 214 CLR 118,
 138
Freeman v Harris [1980] VR 267,
 140
fresh evidence, **143**
Frost v AMACA (2004) 61 NSWLR 158
 (CA), **139**
Fullagar J, **114**, **164**
Fullarton SC, **44**
Furze v Nixon (2000) 2 VR 503 (CA),
 139

G v DPP [1998] QB 919, 21
GAS v The Queen (2004) 217 CLR 198,
132
gender-neutral language, 153
Geraghty J, 164
gerunds, 154
Goddard, Lord, 121, 162
Goldsmith v Sandilands (2002) 76 ALJR
1024, 110
good character, 46, 134
good habits, 7
Gorman, Eugene, 69
Graham Barclay Oysters Pty Ltd v Ryan
(2002) 211 CLR 540, 160
graphics, 15
Grey v The Queen (2001) 75 ALJR
1708, 30
Griffiths, Lord, 164
Griggs case, 124, 126
grounds of appeal, 22
see appeals
guilt
advocate's opinion of, 9
pleading decision, 131
Gummow J, 150
Gumurdul v Reinke (2006) 161 A Crim
R 87, 135

H Clark (Doncaster) Ltd v Wilkinson
[1965] Ch 694, 21
habits, good, 7
handling of witnesses, 5
Harley v McDonald [1999] 3 NZLR
545, 9
Harmony Shipping Co v Davis [1979] 1
All ER 177 (CA), 16
Harmony Shipping Co v Saudi Europe
Line Ltd [1979] 1 WLR 1380, 16
Harris case, 140
Hastings, Patrick, 31, 61, 83
Hatziparadissis v GFC Manufacturing
Co [1978] VR 181, 98
Hawkins v The Queen (1994) 181 CLR
440, 108
Herbert, Shane, 120
Herbert, Siobhan, 83
Hewart CJ, 32

HG v The Queen (1999) 197 CLR 414,
77
Hinz v Berry [1970] 2 QB 40, 162
Hoch v The Queen (1988) 165 CLR 292,
19, 109, 114
homely examples, 126
honesty, 3, 4, 7, 10
see also misleading statements
hostile witnesses, 27
Hrysikos v Mansfield (2002) 5 VR 485,
88, 90, 97, 98
humour, restraint in, 144
Humphreys, Christmas, 121

identification
evidence of, 56
failure of, 68
mistakes in, 26
impaired intelligence, 133
inadmissible evidence
avoiding, 41
documents as, 90
from experts, 77
index
of cases, 13
of law topics, 7
of transcript, 22
Indian Evidence Act 1872, 88
ineffectual questions, 32
insurance investigators, 23, 26
intended comments, 33
interpreters for witnesses, 34
invention, 73
Isaacs, Rufus, 102
issues, one to each question, 29

J Boag & Son Brewing Ltd v Bridon
Investments Pty Ltd (2001) 10
Tas R 26, 89, 90, 98
Jenkins v The Queen (2004) 79 ALJR
252, 27
Jenkinson J, 150
Jones v Hyde (1989) ALJR 349,
143
judges
in appeal courts, 144, 145
attention to, 9

judges (*cont.*)
  complaints about, 141
  grounds for appeal against, 137
  may halt or curtail
      cross-examination, 50
  on cross-examination, 48
  preparation for, 11
  role of, 4
judgment, 4

Kirby J, 138, 159
  on appeals, 146
  Greek reference, 160
  on written submissions, 147,
      149
knowledge
  of human affairs, 124
  importance of, 7
Koutsouridis case, 164

Langdale v Danby [1982] 1 WLR 1123,
      21
language, use of, 1, 3, 4, 8, 147
  see also legal writing
  in examination-in-chief, 41
  by interpreters, 34
  non-English speaking witnesses, 34
  non-English terms, 160
  simple English, 27, 149
Latin, avoiding use of, 28, 160
law, keeping up with, 7
Lawrence, Geoffrey, 94
leading questions, 31
  in cross-examination, 53
  in examination-in-chief, 37
  may unsettle witnesses, 39
  in re-examination, 103
  with opponent's consent, 45
learning, 5
leave to appeal, 144
legal writing 147
  see also language, use of
level of detail, 37
Lewis v The Queen (1987) 88 FLR 104,
      45
lies, 26
  see misleading statements

listening
  to judges, 145
  to witnesses, 34, 38
litigation, requirements for, 18
logic, 8, 109
Lowe v The Queen (1984) 154 CLR 606,
      134
luck, 22
Luxton v Vines (1952) 85 CLR 352, 112

MacPherson v The Queen (1981) 147
      CLR 512, 19, 114
Madison v Goldrick (1976) 1 NSWLR
      651, 89
Makita (Australia) Pry Ltd v Sprowles
      (2001) 52 NSWLR 705, 40, 76,
      77, 80
Marlowe v The Queen (2000) 113 A
      Crim R 118, 105
Martin, Brian, 103
Mason CJ, 144
materials, 16
Maugham, W. Somerset, 148
Maxwell, George, 77, 124, 126
McDermott v The King (1948) 76 CLR
      501, 18, 65
McDermott, Frederick, 18, 66
McHugh J, 153
  on advocacy, 1
  on credibility, 110
  on demeanour, 142
  on examination-in-chief, 38
  written judgements of, 163
Mechanical Inventions v Austin [1935]
      AC 346, 48
medical reports, 16
Meerabux v Attorney-General of Belize
      [2005] 2 AC 513, 141
Meerabux, George, 141
memory, refreshing, 43, 89
Meredith v Innes (1931) 31 SR (NSW)
      104, 106
metaphors, overworked, 161
Mickelberg v The Queen (1989) 167
      CLR 259, 143
Miller v Jackson [1977] 1 QB 966, 162
misleading statements, 26, 57

mistakes made by witnesses, **26, 79**
Mitchell v The Queen (1998) 20 WAR 201, **134**
Mitchell v The Queen (1998) 20 WAR 257, **134**
mitigation, pleas in, **129**
Mollison, Dr., **126**
Mooney v James [1949] VLR 22, **31**
Muir, Richard, **18**
Muirhead J, **125**

negative questions, **29**
negotiating the lowest charge, **131**
Nelson v Chute (1994) 72 A Crim R 85, **133**
newspaper reports, **16**
Ngulkurr v O'Brien (1989) 98 FLR 279, **133**
Nicholls v The Queen (2005) 219 CLR 196, **5, 19, 97, 108**
night work, **22**
Nominal Defendant v Clements (1960) 104 CLR 476, **105**
nominative case, **152**
non-English languages, **160**
Norrish, Stephen, **82**
North London Railway Co v Great North Railway Co (1883) 11 QBD 30, **149**
notes
    for closing address, **123**
    made during case, **22**
    making, **13**
    summaries of, **20**
    taken by witnesses, **43, 85**
    when to avoid taking, **52**
Nudd v The Queen (2006) 80 ALJR 614, **7**
numbers, correct use of, **157**

O'Gorman, Dan, **81**
O'Leary v The King (1946) 73 CLR 566, **112**
objections
    to evidence, **19, 113**
    to forms of questions, **115**
objective case, **152**

observation, need for, **3**
occupation of witness, ascertaining, **39**
'one question too many', **59**
Opas, Phillip, **78**
opening addresses, **120**
opinion evidence, **17, 76**
order of examination-in-chief, **42**
overworked metaphors, **161**

padding, avoiding, **30, 160**
Palmer v The Queen (1998) 193 CLR 1, **38, 108, 110**
Pangaraminni, Regis, **101**
parity in sentencing, **134**
participial phrases, **150**
parties, **165**
    see clients
Pearce v The Queen (1998) 194 CLR 610, **134**
perfection not possible, **10**
personal pronouns, **152**
pettifoggery, **142**
Pfennig v The Queen (1995) 182 CLR 461, **109**
photograph albums, **15**
physique, requirements of, **3**
platitudes, **161**
Plato Films Ltd v Speidel [1961] AC 1090 (HL), **46**
pleading, decision on, **131**
pleas in mitigation, **129**
pleonasms, **159**
plurals, correct use of, **156**
police
    notes taken by, **44**
    statements taken by, **23, 26**
    as witnesses, **25**
politeness, **159**
    see courtesy
Pollard v The Queen (1992) 176 CLR 177, **5**
Pollitt v The Queen (1992) 174 CLR 558, **27**
Porter, Chester, **18, 24**
positivity in writing, **148**
Powell case, **149**
practiced witnesses, **25**

precedent in appeals, **145**
preparation, **11**
  for appeals, **138**
  for closing address, **124**
  for court attendance, **165**
  for cross-examination, **20**
  overnight, **22**
  for pleas in mitigation, **130**,
    134
  for writing submissions, **148**
prepositions, **152**
presence, need for, **3**
pre-trial documents, **23**
previous convictions, **70**
previous inconsistent statement, **92**
prior consistent statement,
    93
prior convictions, **132**
prior inconsistent statement, **92**
procedure, rules of, **8**
pronouns, **152**
proof
  of death, **21**
  of the case, **36**
  onus of, **110**
  of the witness, **38**
prosecution, closing address, **123**
provenance of exhibits, **14**
psychiatric difficulties, **133**
Putti v Simpson (1975) 6 ALR 47, **11**,
    130

qualities of advocacy, **1**
Queen's Case (1820) 2 Brod & Bing
    284, **88**, **97**
Queensberry, Marquess of, **17**, 61
questions, 55
  see also leading questions
  in cross-examination, **55**
  excessive, **59**
  forms of, **40**
  from witnesses, **24**
  to witnesses, **23**, **27**
quotations, use of, **163**

R (Jackson) v Attorney-General [2006]
    1 AC 262, **8**

R (on the application of Lynch) v
    General Dental Council [2004] 1
    All ER 1159, **164**
R (McCann) v Manchester Crown Court
    [2003] 1 AC 787, **141**
R v Abusafiah (1991) 24 NSWLR 531,
    111
R v AJS (2005) 159 A Crim R 327, **100**,
    103, **106**
R v Alexander and McKenzie (2002) 6
    VR 53, **91**
R v Alexander and Taylor [1975] VR
    741, **44**
R v Amad [1962] VR 545, **5**
R v Anderson (1929) 21 Cr App R 178,
    62, **88**, **97**
R v Anderson (1991) 1 NTLR 149, **5**,
    51, **51**, **108**, **114**
R v B [1966] 1 WLR 1612, **142**
R v Bajic (2005) 154 A Crim R 196,
    153
R v Balchin (1974) 9 SASR 64, **22**
R v Baldwin [1925] All ER Rep, **33**
R v Banks (1916) 12 Cr App R 74, **98**
R v Banner [1970] VR 240, **114**
R v Basha (1989) 39 A Crim R 337, **19**,
    113
R v Bedington [1970] Qd R 353, **90**, **91**,
    98
R v Birks (1990) 19 NSWLR 677, **5**, **22**,
    48
R v Bliss [1937] 1 DLR 1, **131**
R v Bridger [2003] 1 NZLR 636, **133**
R v Brownlow (2003) 86 SASR 114
    (CCA), **159**
R v Burns (2003) 137 A Crim R 557
    (NSW CCA), **59**
R v Bux (2002) 132 A Crim R 395, **133**
R v C (1993) 60 SASR 467, **77**
R v Calder [1987] 1 Qd R 62 (CCA),
    160
R v Carroll (2002) 213 CLR 635, **154**
R v Champion (1992) 64 A Crim R 244,
    133
R v Chandu Nagrecha [1997] 2 Cr App
    R 401, **19**
R v Chayna (1993) 66 A Crim R 178, **82**

R v Chen and Others (2002) 130 A
Crim R 300, **39**, **44**

R v Chin (1985) 157 CLR 671, **117**

R v Christie [1914] AC 545, **108**

R v Churchill, August 1999 (Western
Australian Supreme Court),
123

R v Clarke (2001) 123 A Crim R 506
(NSW CCA), **27**

R v Cooper (1985) 82 Cr App R 74, **98**

R v Cooper (Supreme Court of
Queensland), **82**

R v Coventry (1997) 7 Tas R 199, **31**

R v Craig and Bentley, 9 December
1952, **121**

R v Crehan and Rowe (2001) 4 VR 189
(CA), **140**

R v Crippen, Oct 18–22, 1910, **69**, **70**

R v DAH (2004) 150 A Crim R 14 (SA
CCA), **33**

R v David [1966] VR 358, **131**

R v Doheny and Adams [1997] 1 Cr
App R 369, **8**

R v Donald (1983) 34 SASR 10, **114**,
141

R v Dowlan [1998] 1 VR 123, **134**

R v Einem (No 2) (1991) 52 A Crim R
402, **54**

R v F (1995) 83 A Crim R 502, **77**

R v Fish and Swan (2002) 131 A Crim R
172, **68**, **104**

R v Foggo; Ex parte Attorney-General
[1989] 2 Qd R 49, **90**, **98**

R v Fowler (2003) 151 A Crim R 166,
29, **142**

R v François [1994] 2 SCR 827, **40**

R v Fraser (1995) 65 SASR 260, **89**, **97**,
105, **109**

R v Fuge (2001) 123 A Crim R 310, **142**

R v Funderburk [1990] 1 WLR 587, **19**

R v Gardner, February 1989 (Victorian
Supreme Court), **123**

R v Georgiev (2001) 119 A Crim R 363,
106

R v Gibb and McKenzie [1983] 2 VR
155, **73**

R v Glossop [2001] NSWCCA 165, **83**

R v Govinden (1999) 106 A Crim R 314
(NSW CCA), **129**

R v Green (2002) 4 VR 471, **137**

R v Griggs (Supreme Court of Victoria,
Sale, 7 March 1928), **78**, **126**

R v Handy [2002] 2 SCR 908, **112**

R v Hanrahan (1964) 87 WN (NSW)
458, **72**

R v Harmer (1985) 28 A Crim R 35, **109**

R v Harris (1988) 17 NSWLR 158, **140**

R v Harrison [1966] VR 72, **89**, **98**

R v Haycraft (1974) 54 Cr App R 121
(CCA), **142**

R v Higgins (1994) 71 A Crim R 429, **50**

R v Hircock [1970] 1 QB 67, **4**

R v Hoad (1989) 42 A Crim R 312 (Qld
CCA), **159**

*R v Horseferry Road Magistrates' Court;
Ex parte Bennett* [1994] 1 AC
42, **164**

R v Howes (2000) 2 VR 141, **152**

R v Hughes (Supreme Court of
Victoria) 17 July 1990, **21**, **81**

R v Hughes (Vic CCA 20 March 1990,
unreported), **45**

R v Hutchinson (1990) 53 SASR 587
(CCA), **27**

R v Jack (1894) 15 LR (NSW) 196, **89**,
97

R v Johnson (2001) 126 A Crim R 395,
30

R v Karger (2002) 83 SASR 135, **8**

R v Kehagias [1985] VR 107, **106**

R v King [1983] 1 WLR 411; 1 All ER
929, **16**

R v King (2004) 150 A Crim R 409, **55**

R v Kirk [2000] 1 WLR 567, **4**

R v KJ (2005) 154 A Crim R 139 (Vic
CA), **160**

R v Knight & Ors, February 2000, **124**

R v Kolalich (1990) 47 A Crim R 71, **131**

R v Kostaras (No 2) (2003) 86 SASR
541, **55**

R v Kotzmann (No 2) (2002) 128 A
Crim R 479, **159**

R v Koutsouridis (1982) 7 A Crim R
237, **114**, **164**

R v Lars and Others (1994) 73 A Crim R 91, **34**

R v Lavery (1979) 20 SASR 430, **141**

R v Le (2002) 130 A Crim R 44, **33**

R v Le (2002) 54 NSWLR 474 (CCA), **27**

R v Lewis (2003) 142 A Crim R 254 (NSW CCA), **160**

R v Lewis-Hamilton [1998] 1 VR 630, **17**

R v Madden (1999) 85 A Crim R 385 (NSW CCA), **140**

R v Mahoney (2000) 114 A Crim R 130, **142**

R v Markulesi (2001) 52 NSWLR 82, **38, 104**

R v Martin (No 2) (1997) 68 SASR 419, **40, 74**

R v Mason [1988] 1 WLR 139, **108**

R v Matthews [1960] 1 SA 752, **109**

R v McConville (Supreme Court of Victoria), **62, 63, 67, 92**

R v McFadden (1975) 62 Cr App R 187, **9**

R v McGregor [1984] 1 Qd R 256, **89, 90**

R v McIntyre (2000) 111 A Crim R 211 (NSW CCA), **10**

R v Minani (2005) 154 A Crim R 347 (NSW CCA), **160**

R v Minister for Immigration and Cultural Affairs; Ex parte 5154 (2003) 77 ALJR 1909, **154**

R v Moore (1995) 77 A Crim R 577, **89**

R v Morgan [1976] AC 182, **111**

R v Morris [1951] 1 KB 394, **162**

R v Murphy (1985) 4 NSWLR 42, **46**

R v Musolino (2003) 86 SASR 37, **97**

R v Ncanana [1948] 4 SALR 399, **27**

R v Newton (2002) 128 A Crim R 185 (SA CCA), **160**

R v Nguyen [1998] 4 VR 394, **143**

R v Nicholas (2000) 111 A Crim R 490, **160**

R v NJM (2001) 126 A Crim R 378, **73**

R v NRC [1999] 3 VR 537 (CA), **48**

R v Okutgen (1982) 8 A Crim R 262, **134**

R v Olbrich (1999) 199 CLR 270, **132**

R v Orton [1922] VLR 469, **28, 91, 98**

R v Parker and Mulhall (2002) 131 A Crim R 597, **131**

R v Pearce [1953] Tas LR 69, **131**

R v Powell (2001) 81 SASR 9 (CCA), **149**

R v Previtera (1997) 94 A Crim R 76, **134**

R v Quentin Tipungwuti (Northern Territory Supreme Court, Darwin), **67**

R v Ready and Manning [1942] VLR 85, **106**

R v Richardson [1969] 1 QB 299, **72**

R v Rose [1998] 3 SCR 262, **122**

R v Rowe (2004) 50 NSWLR 510 (CCA), **140**

R v Rowton (1865) Le & Ca 520, **46**

R v Rugari (2001) 122 A Crim R 1, **159**

R v Ryan, **79**

R v Sandford (1994) 37 NSWLR 172, **19, 114**

R v Sang [1980] AC 402, **108**

R v Santos and Carrion (1987) 45 SASR 556, **101**

R v Saragozza [1984] VR 118, **111**

R v Sargent [2003] 1 AC 347, **4**

R v Seham Yousry (1914) 11 Cr App R 13, **90, 98**

R v Sharp [1994] QB 261, **48**

R v Shaw [1996] 1 Qd R 641, **37**

R v Smith (1982) 7 A Crim R 437, **134**

R v Smith [1992] 2 SCR 915, **4**

R v Smith (No 2) (1995) 64 SASR 1, **105**

R v Solomon (2005) 153 A Crim R 32, **155**

R v Soma (2003) 212 CLR 299, **92, 98, 117**

R v Stephenson [1976] VR 376, **109**

R v Stokes and Difford (1990) 51 A Crim R 25 (NSW CCA), **22**

R v Symons (1988) 32 A Crim R 370, **78**

R v Szach (1980) 23 SASR 504, **103**

R v Taktak (1988) 14 NSWLR 226, **79**

R v Talia [1996] 1 VR 462, **134**

R v Teys (2001) 161 FLR 44, **32**

R v Thomas (2006) 163 A Crim R 567, **137**

R v Tierney (1990) 51 A Crim R 446 (Vic CCA), **159**

R v Tipungwuti (Northern Territory Supreme Court), 66, 84, 101, **127**

R v Titijewski [1970] VR 371, **106**

R v Trotter (1982) 7 A Crim R 8, **90**, **91**, **98**

R v Tsiaras [1996] 1 VR 398, **133**

R v Umanski [1961] VR 242, **5**, **52**, **116**

R v Vent (1935) 25 Cr App R 55, **131**

R v Ward (1981) 3 A Crim R 171 (NSW CCA), **16**

R v Warren (1994) 72 A Crim R 74, **21**

R v Weatherstone (1968) 12 FLR 14, **89**

R v White (1997) 32 OR (3d) 722, **7**

R v Williams [2001] 1 Qd R 212, **28**

R v Wood & Ors (1996) 87 A Crim R 346 (Qld CA), **152**

R v Yaldiz [1998] 2 VR 396, **133**

Randwick Corporation v Rutledge (1959) 102 CLR 54, **151**

Rawcliffe v The Queen (2000) 22 WAR 490, **103**

Re Anne Hamilton-Byrne [1995] 1 VR 129 (FC), **140**

Re Hallett's Estate (1880) 13 Ch D 696, **145**

reasons for witnesses' actions, **104**

rebutting recent invention, **105**

recent invention, **73**, **105**

re-examination, **100**

refreshing memory, **43**, **89**

relevance, **19**, **50**, **108**

reputation
    evidence as to, **72**
    good character, **117**

requirements for litigation, **18**

Revesz v The Queen (1996) 88 A Crim R 253, **21**

reviving witnesses' credit, **106**

right of reply, **37**

Riley J, **101**

Robinson v The Queen (2006) 162 A Crim R 88, **4**

Rondel v Worsley [1969] 1 AC 191, **10**

rules of evidence, **8**

Russell, Charles, **53**

Ryder v Hartford Insurance Co [1977] VR 257, **150**

Saunders v The Queen (1985) 15 A Crim R 115, **37**

sayings, **161**

scenes of activity, visiting, **17**

Schreiner JA, **109**

Scopes, John, **34**

Scragg, Gregory, **79**

Senat v Senat [1965] P 172, **89**, **98**

Seneviratne v The King [1936] 3 All ER 36 (PC), **24**

senior advocates, learning from, **6**

sentencing, appeal against, **137**

settling the facts, **132**

Shand, Jack, **18**, **57**

Shepherd v The Queen (1990) 170 CLR 573, **112**

Shorey v PT Ltd (2003) 77 ALJR 1104, **85**

short sentences, **149**

side issues, **12**

Simon, Viscount, **114**

simple English, **27**
    see also language, use of
    in examination-in-chief, **41**
    word choice, **149**

simple examples, **80**

Skinner, Dr., **82**

slang, use of, **27**

Smith v The Queen (2001) 206 CLR 650, **19**, **50**, **77**, **108**

Smith, T.W., **85**

Southwood J, **163**

split infinitives, **156**

starting a witness, **41**

statements
    see witness statements

statutory law, appeals under, **138**

Stevens v The Queen (2005) 80 ALJR 91, **163**

Stirland v Director of Public Prosecutions
[1944] AC 315, **114, 141**
Stonehouse case, **122**
stopping a witness, **41**
stopping cross-examination, **59**
Stronach, Nurse, **94**
style
in cross-examination, **60**
style, developing, **7**
subjunctive mood, **151**
submissions, **89, 116**
see also legal writing
to DPP, **131**
written, increasing demand for, **147**
Sutton v Derschaw & Ors (1995) 82 A
Crim R 318, **54**
Sutton v The Queen (1984) 152 CLR
528, **109**
Sweeney v Fitzhardinge (1906) 4 CLR
716, **138**

telephone records, **16**
The Waterways Authority v Fitzgibbon
(2005) 79 ALJR 1816, **102**
Thomas v The Queen (1960) 102 CLR
584, **151**
Thompson v The King [1918] AC 221,
111
Thompson v The Queen (2005) 157 A
Crim R 385, **133**
tightening the net, **58**
timing, **31**
Tipungwuti, Quentin, **66**
see R v Tipungwuti (Northern
Territory Supreme Court)
Tomlins v Brennan (2006) 18 NTLR 80,
163
toning down weak points, **45**
totality, **134**
Tractor Joe, **84**
training, **5**
transcript, index to, **22**
true appeals, **138**
turning the witness your way, **82**

undermining witnesses, **63, 91**
unfair hearing submission, **116**

unfavourable witnesses, **27**
Uniform Evidence Acts (Cth, NSW &
Tas), 27, **88, 91**

Van Den Hoek v The Queen (1987) 28 A
Crim R 424, **42**
Veen v The Queen [No 2] (1988) 164
CLR 465, **133, 155**
verbosity
see language, use of
verbs, correct use of, **156**
Vesey v Bus Eireann [2001] 4 IR 192,
49
Vetrovec v The Queen [1982] 1 SCR
811, **27**
victims of crime, **133**
Vizzard, Frederick, **65**
vocal qualities, **3**
voir dire, **19, 113**

Wakeley v The Queen (1990) 64 ALJR
321, **51**
Walker v Walker (1937) 57 CLR 630,
89
Wallin v Curtain (1998) 100 A Crim R
506 (Vic CA), **139**
Walsh QC, **41**
Walsh v Law Society of New South Wales
(1999) 198 CLR 73, **155**
Walters J, **141**
Warren, Samuel, **57**
watching judges, **145**
watching witnesses, **34, 38, 52**
weak points, **45**
weakening evidence, **49**
Weininger v The Queen (2003) 212 CLR
629, **132**
Wheelahan, Dennis, **102**
Whisprun Pty Ltd v Dixon (2003) 77
ALJR 1598, **141**
Whitehorn v The Queen (1983) 152
CLR 657, **4, 24**
Whitlam v ASIC (2003) 199 ALR 674,
103
Wilde, Oscar, **17, 61**
Williams v Spautz (1992) 174 CLR 509,
116

wisdom, **4**
wit, need for, **3**
witness statements, **13**, **14**, **23**, **26**, **38**
    see also proof
witnesses
    see also re-examination,
        cross-examination
    agreeable, **73**
    arguing with, **30**
    attention to, **34**, **38**, **52**
    backgrounds of, **17**
    children as, **20**, **73**
    choosing, **23**
    defence witnesses, **36**
    establishing credentials, **77**
    ethical treatment of, **165**
    examination-in-chief, **41**
    handling of, **5**
    index of, **13**
    keeping control of, **55**

    questions and, **23**
    reasons for actions, **104**
    reviving credit of, **106**
    setting at ease, **39**
    statements by, **16**
    turning your way, **82**
    undermining, **63**, **91**
Wood v Desmond (1958) 78 WN 65, **88**,
    97
Woods v Rogers; Ex parte Wood [1983] 2
    Qd R 212, **114**, **142**
*Woolmington v Director of Public
    Prosecutions* [1935] AC 462,
    111
words
    see also language, use of
    correct use of, **149**, **154**

York v The Queen (2005) 225 CLR 466,
    153